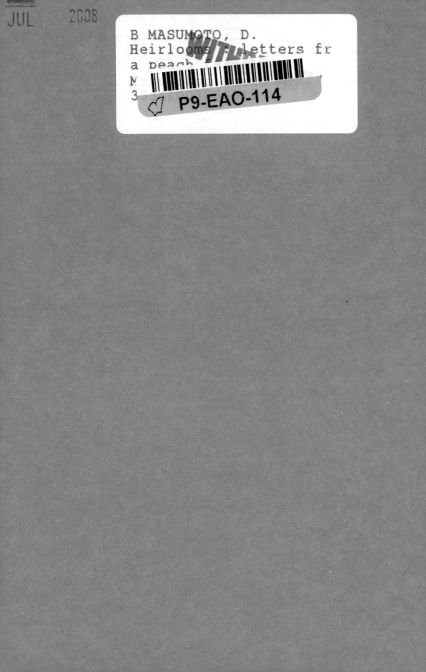

Heirlooms

LETTERS FROM A PEACH FARMER

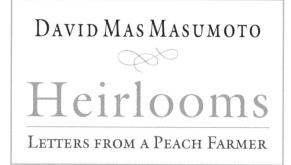

DAVID MAS MASUMOTO

Heirlooms

LETTERS FROM A PEACH FARMER

ILLUSTRATED BY DOUG HANSEN

GREAT VALLEY BOOKS

HEYDAY BOOKS, BERKELEY, CALIFORNIA

Library of Congress Cataloging-in-Publication Data

Masumoto, David Mas.
  Heirlooms : letters from a peach farmer / David Mas Masumoto ; illustrated by Doug Hansen.
    p. cm. -- (Great valley books)
  ISBN 978-1-59714-064-5 (hardcover : alk. paper)
  1. Masumoto, David Mas--Correspondence. 2. Farmers--California--Del Rey--Biography. 3. Japanese American farmers--California--Del Rey--Biography. 4. Farm life--California--Del Rey. 5. Family farms--California--Del Rey. I. Title.
  SB63.M36A3 2007
  630.92--dc22
  [B]
                                    2007003256

Cover Art: Doug Hansen
Cover and Interior Design/Typesetting: Lorraine Rath
Printed in Malaysia by Imago

Orders, inquiries, and correspondence should be addressed to:
        Heyday Books
        P. O. Box 9145, Berkeley, CA 94709
        (510) 549-3564, Fax (510) 549-1889
        www.heydaybooks.com

10 9 8 7 6 5 4 3 2 1

CONTENTS

Introduction

Dear Reader,

A letter.

A hug with words.

People matter in letters—that is part of the personal nature of correspondence. A letter starts with "Dear," a serious word about caring.

Today, letters still count. Even with high technology, the Internet, cell phones, text messaging, and computers, one major means of communication has become e-mail. Old-fashioned letter writing. Words still matter. A simple truth remains: good writing gets read and answered first.

Beyond that, good letters reflect good thinking. I believe when you write, you have to think first, then communicate. I've never seen written in a letter "Sorry, I didn't mean to say that." I hope my letters are about reflection, then expression.

These thirty letters are essays for a monthly column I've been writing since 2002 for the *Fresno Bee* in California's Central Valley. The first two years are collected in a book called *Letters to the Valley, A Harvest of Memories* (Heyday Books, 2004). The last three years are collected here.

My first editor at the *Fresno Bee,* Charlie Waters, said that a good column is like a letter to a friend. I took that to heart. Letter writing: the simple act of committing thoughts to words; capturing observations and feelings; sharing them with others so they may be read and reread. If my letters work, I leave behind a piece of myself.

In these essays, you'll read about my passion for farming. I grew up on a small, eighty-acre family farm outside of Fresno. Like many farm kids, I ran off to college (the University of California, Berkeley) hoping to escape the slow life out in the country. The two hundred miles from the farm to college were not enough, and I then journeyed to Japan as an exchange student, living there for two years, only to discover what I missed: the open countryside, the land, and her people, my family and community. I came back to farm organically, returning to our peaches, nectarines, grapes, and raisins.

I became a native son, drawn back to a place my grandparents desperately wanted to call home after they had immigrated to the U.S. from Japan in the early 1900s. I learned the sense of place my parents had forged. They grew up working the land of the Central Valley, then were uprooted during World War II when all Japanese Americans were forcibly removed and imprisoned in relocation camps because they looked like the enemy. After the war, my parents came back to the only place they knew as home.

I hope to leave my mark and leave behind stories. I hope people want to know more about where their food comes from, how it's grown, and who grows it. I believe people still have a memory of the real flavors of a juicy summer peach and luscious nectarine. This is not just a farm, it's about farming organically and facing the challenges of working with nature.

Writing a column exposes my family and myself. My private thoughts go public as I hope to connect with the reader. My best work goes beyond the surface and into real emotions—things you'd share with a good friend.

My family lies at the heart of many of my stories. My wife, Marcy, knows farm life. Her doctorate in education masks her upbringing on a goat dairy in the high desert of southern California, where her family had transplanted rural traditions from Wisconsin. Our daughter, Nikiko, a teenager when I started my columns and now a college student, escaped the slow rhythms of our valley and yet is also lured back by the siren of the farm, the land, and her people. Our son, Korio, a teenager who works summers with peaches, knows all too well of his father's work. Farmers can't keep secrets; our work is public.

The Central Valley of California is a four-hundred-mile-long, fifty-mile-wide ancient lakebed. The topsoil is rich; our dirt has the light flavor of sandy loam, perfect for grapes and stone fruit. The mountains of the Sierra Nevada tower to the east and capture snows for spring and summer irrigation. Without that water, our land would be a desert, struggling to grow much beyond prairie grasses with our annual rainfall of about ten inches. The summers are dry and hot with sweat, an inescapable fact in a place well suited for peaches and nectarines. My fruits love the heat and arid climate, similar to their origins in the high deserts of China.

I've often thought of this valley as a series of villages connected by an asphalt river called Highway 99. We live with our shortcomings, accept imperfections with a simple and naive perspective. We claim to be a comfortable place to raise families and grow old. Good enough to call home. But life is changing with rapid population growth and a shift away from agrarian economies. Twenty miles north of our small farm, Fresno has grown to a half-million people and planners project that this area will be home to over a million within my lifetime. A million neighbors. A million stories.

I've tried to collect a few stories here. Divided into five sections, each explores the life and rhythms of this valley, our farm, my neighbors and family. All are part of a geography of place, stories from "the other California," not northern California dominated by San Francisco and the Bay Area, not "So-Cal" and the life of Los Angeles. Too often we have been invisible. But a new energy is growing here in the valley, a land where the embedded traditions face a future of change. And that's good.

I hope my letters convey my belief that anything in life worth doing must be done with passion. I try to choose my words carefully, write stories with conviction. I journey with words and hope my stories travel beyond our valley. Yet in the end, I believe life is simply about loving. And loving words.

Thanks for listening and reading.

Mas

To my parents and Marcy, Nikiko, and Korio
—David Mas Masumoto

To June Elaine Victoria Pool
—Doug Hansen

PART ONE

Memories

Grandmother's Letters

Dear Dad,

When did you realize your mother could not read or write? As a child, I assumed most everyone could read books or signs, could write a simple note or letter. I never thought of the challenge immigrants like *Baachan* (Grandmother) faced.

Being illiterate robbed her of a sense, like becoming blind or losing your hearing or ability to touch and feel. Especially being a foreigner, she may have always felt that without written language skills in either Japanese or English, something was missing. Words could have completed her.

Baachan grew up on a small farm in southern Japan. A young girl back then wasn't expected to stay in school. She was destined to work in the fields and raise a family. When the price of their rice crops fell and her father suddenly died, her younger brother inherited the farm. As a teenager, she needed to find a home. A marriage was arranged. With the hope of a better life, she immigrated to America to meet a husband.

I remember a bundle of letters Baachan kept tucked

safely away in the back of her dresser drawer. They were wrapped in a faded, white muslin cloth. A dull, tan string, with frayed ends, securely bound the collection together. The envelopes had yellowed and felt brittle. Some were written in English. Others had funny squiggly lines and strokes created with black ink.

When I was a youngster, the Japanese kanji appeared both strange and mysterious. They were written in a vertical line moving from right to left. I remember watching a few old Issei men, first-generation Japanese in America, read letters and Japanese newspapers. Their eyes moved up and down and heads seemed to nod as they read, completing one line and moving back up to the next. The complex series of strokes and dashes carried hidden messages, information from a distant homeland, news from native villages, words from faraway families.

I never recall Baachan reading any of her letters. Clearly she valued them, keeping them stored with her alien registration card and the Purple Heart from the U.S. Army after her oldest son died fighting in France during World War II. Without translation, though, all the writing—either in English or Japanese—must have appeared as dark scratches on pieces of paper. Why would she keep something she could never read?

As a teenager, I discovered she couldn't write. I planned to journey to Japan as an exchange student and wanted to learn how to write our family name in Japanese. I sat down with Baachan, produced some pencils and blank white paper, and mumbled a few Japanese words I knew. "*Namae* (name)," I asked. "*Namae kudasai* (please)." I pointed to the writing instruments and smiled at her.

She blinked back, her seventy-year-old eyes dull. I gently pushed a pencil into her old, calloused hand, gesturing her to write. Since my Japanese language skills were so bad, I knew I couldn't ask much more. She awkwardly squeezed the slender wood and it slipped from her bony fingers.

I picked it up and again placed it in her hand. Her old hand shook as she gamely tried to write. Her fingers turned white as she gripped the pencil tightly. The lead point pierced the paper and tore through, leaving behind a few rough scratches and a hole. She put the pencil down and looked away.

Baachan could not write her name. Later, I learned she could not read. I then thought of those close family friends who'd come visit and Baachan would have them read the letters out loud. I thought they were just sharing information. These were educated individuals who read and wrote letters and documents for a community.

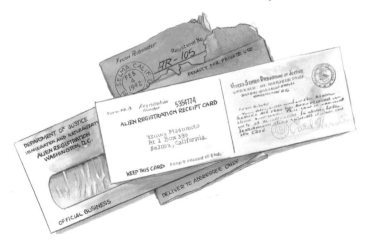

Dad, you were the first generation of our family to become literate in English. It probably didn't feel like a big deal yet it remains significant. An act that now seems simple embodied a powerful symbol. Immigrant families share rites of passage. Was learning to read a new language the first step in calling a place home? Was learning to write your name a part of making their mark in a new land?

❧

Some high school students wrote me a handful of letters. They described how their families were often like ours, immigrants to the Valley. Some worked in the fields, all struggled to find a place where they belonged. Many also had family who could not read nor write.

One young Latina wrote about her own grandmother. The granddaughter gave a birthday card to her grandmother and asked her to read it out loud, but the old woman refused. The teenager asked why. The grandmother didn't say a word, and then started crying.

"Why you cry?" asked the granddaughter.

The grandmother asked her not to tell anyone and said she didn't know how to read. Tears came out.

"What about all the other cards and letters I wrote you?" asked the granddaughter. They were saved in a box.

The granddaughter was shocked. Then, wonderfully, she decided to teach her grandmother how to read and write.

These stories make our valley special, simple tales about the basic things many take for granted. Buried in the data about our schools, lost in the demographics about our population, masked behind terms like "English language learners," lie stories about generations opening a new world of language and words. For some, families, not individuals, become literate. An accomplishment to celebrate and not conceal with shame.

When we learn to read and write we leave a mark on the places we call home. Perhaps Baachan would have felt complete when our family could read a story about the place where they learned to write their names. That's why she still clung to that handful of letters, scratches that carried meaning and memories for another generation. Some of our families require generations to learn and fully understand letters.

Your son,
Mas

Scouting Uniforms

Dear Bob,

We weren't the best Boy Scouts, out motley group of mostly seventh and eighth graders from Del Rey Elementary School. Our troop was formed in 1967 and lasted for about two years before we wore everyone out. It was an innocent time for a sleepy farm town—actually a farmworker town back then, and still is. The revolution of that decade never quite made it to Del Rey.

Our troop reflected who we were, the demographics quite representative of Del Rey: 60 to 70 percent "Mexicans" and the rest a few white kids like you and a few Japanese Americans like me. Bob, we didn't know it, but we were poor and no one was wealthy.

Those who had fathers with steady jobs, like your dad, or my father, who had a farm, were considered rich, although there were years on the farm when the workers made more money than the farmer. We both naively believed our classmates were world travelers, annually journeying to such foreign places as Texas and Mexico in the late fall and returning in the spring.

Our troop was a "cause" supported by the Del Rey Lions

Club, a group of mostly Anglo men with good hearts who felt sorry for us—youth who they believed were destined for trouble. The Boy Scouts could reform us, "keep us off the streets," train us to become good boys, while tossing in some patriotism and honor. After our group had met for a few months, most of us realized Scouting was great for a boring little town with nothing to do.

Of course, none of us really knew what Scouting was all about. We had no idea it was formed as a program for young boys and based on a military model of discipline, outdoor skill training, and codes of conduct. You know, Bob, those skills we supposedly needed to become men.

If we had understood what Scouting was supposed to be, most of us would have quit and laughed at the noble but misguided paternalism, or we would have consciously lied and deceived leaders, making them think we bought into a code of honor that made no sense on our dusty streets. All we really wanted was to get out of the fields, with only a few of us (including me) struggling between trying to be a "good American Scout" and the realities of Del Rey.

One moment that seemed to capture the collision of intentions was a Scout Jamboree, one of our first overnight camping trips, on a ranch in the Sanger river-bottom area. I can't recall exactly how we were told to prepare, only that no one quite knew what to bring nor how to pack. We met at the American Legion Hall across from Del Rey School and twenty boys piled into cars for the fifteen-minute drive.

When we arrived, we saw other troops from Sanger, Reedley, Selma, even Fresno. They were unloading their stuff with discipline and organization, their cars were packed neatly and efficiently. I'm sure those Scouts screwed around a lot and I know many endured multiple bouts of hazing, the unspoken rites of passage often part of a Boy Scout experience. (In hindsight, maybe it was more like the military than I imagined.)

We arrived in an odd assortment of cars and dusty pick-up trucks. One was a real cool '57 Chevy that Louie's older brother or cousin drove; we fought to ride in that beauty. Other vehicles included a low rider with hydraulics, cherry red and chromed, and still another was a farmworker's family car, properly filled with dust and dirt, two jugs of water on the back seat, and a sweet smell of sweat, a hint of honest work in the fields. We had tossed everything into trucks already filled with junk, including auto repair tools, a barbecue, some pruning shears and oil, along with some chains and pipe kept handy.

We piled out and listened to Juan, our Scoutmaster, give instructions. He was a good-hearted person who wanted to give back to his community. He only had daughters and I sense that he wanted to help train and direct a son. The only problem was that since he never had a son, he had little experience working with young boys.

He lined us up next to the cars, a type of inspection to show our worth. That's when we noticed that no one had a full Boy Scout uniform. In fact, if our troop had a basic uniform, it was a white t-shirt, black pants, slick hair, and black leather shoes. The few pieces of the official gear were scattered throughout the troop. I had a hat and neckerchief with clasp. Bob, you had a shirt and hat but had shared your neckerchief and clasp. Meathead had located a shirt but got mixed up with the wrong color neckerchief, and Danny was the most equipped, just lacking the official Boy Scout stuff from waist down.

I even had an official Scout belt. After seeing pictures in a Scout booklet that showed how a belt could be used in many ways—from an emergency strap to pull yourself off a mountain cliff or as a band to tie together sticks when gathering (that could presumably become a signal fire if you became disoriented in a forest—again, it would save your life), I had convinced my mom that it was something I had to have. She, of course, sagely recognized I could possibly use this for years to come, even out in the fields.

I also had "lent" my handkerchief to Randy; actually, he asked me in a pretty forceful way. Ernie had pulled out a faded blue work handkerchief, the type the farmworkers used to cover their heads or protect their faces, and he tied it around his head like a bandanna. Big Guy had appropriated a cap and Jessie had managed to locate a clasp, wrapping a white handkerchief properly around his white t-shirt.

Dickie had found an old Boy Scout hat, or at least something that looked military. But it was two or three sizes too small for his rather large head, so he wore it slightly angled to the side, like the pictures we had seen of soldiers, hoping he would look cool. Instead it kept sliding off until he gave up and tossed it to Tommy, a little guy who lied about his age in order to join the troop. (No one really paid much attention to how old others were. It was a time when kids actually flunked grades, and a few boys in the sixth grade already had mustaches.)

I suppose if you added all our uniform parts together, we'd more or less outfit four fully dressed Scouts from the waist up. But dispersing them across a gang of twenty boys seemed proper for us kids from Del Rey. It wasn't exactly spreading the wealth: the tougher kids demanded we share and I quickly complied out of fear for my personal safety. And wasn't Scouting about honor and duty and obligation?

At that moment, Bob, I may have begun to realize who we weren't. We were not like the other troops with their official uniforms and packs. We identified more with the Hispanic kids in our troop, and were part of a culture able to adapt to situations and still look exactly the way we should. We had taken the uniform of Scouting and made it our own.

All this right in the middle of the sixties, with battles of race and civil rights swirling around us in this Central Valley. Fifty miles down the road to Delano, Cesar Chavez led the movement to unionize farmworkers, but that could have been a thousand miles away.

So we stood in line for inspection. Other troops were arriving, and I'm sure they laughed when they saw how poorly we were dressed. I suppose they were right, Bob, and yet, this is where you and I belonged.

Your Scouting buddy,
Mas

Marching with Louie

Dear Bob,

Remember our ragtag Boy Scout troop from the poor farmworker town of Del Rey? Late spring, 1967: we had arrived at a Scout Jamboree at a ranch in the Sanger river-bottom area. Our Scoutmaster, Juan, made us line up for inspection, and we must have looked atrocious with a few bits and pieces of Scout uniforms scattered among twenty boys. We were preparing to march into the open field and eventually the campsite about a mile away.

I watched other troops from Fresno and neighboring towns unload their cars. They had tents and neatly packed backpacks in regulation khaki color. Few of us had the right equipment. We carried duffel bags, Army surplus packs, and one small suitcase. Our troop sponsor, the Del Rey Lions Club, had bought us bulky, heavy canvas tents that seemed to weigh a ton.

Other troops had colorful flags with emblems and designs I had seen in the Boy Scout handbook. Bob, didn't you make a "Wolf" patrol banner out of an old bed sheet and a marking pen? And our other patrol—the Thunderbirds—had skillfully spray-painted the black outline of a bird that looked more like the United Farm Workers emblem than anything else. We used a stick to hold our flags up high and proudly.

I didn't pay much attention, though, as I was still frantically trying to tie a thick flannel sleeping bag, which my mom had borrowed from a cousin, to my little backpack. For some reason I had appropriated an extra-long strand of rope from my dad's truck. The farm rope was about three-quarters of an inch thick, extremely strong so it could hold down thousands of pounds of fruit boxes, but hopelessly too fat to tie down my equipment. Meathead suggested I drag my sleeping bag behind me, but Valente came over instead, whipped out a switchblade, cut the rope into more manageable lengths, and saved me.

I also had trouble packing my food. My mom hinted that I should take a "nigiri" (rice ball) for my lunch, but I told her this was the Boy Scouts: "They don't eat rice." So I had jammed a half loaf of Wonder Bread into my pack, only later discovering it had gotten crushed into a cube about two or three inches square.

Most of the other guys were smarter about their food. They brought tortillas: light, compact, and able to withstand a hike. Although I believe Jessie became embarrassed about his food when one of the younger guys, Ernie, began talking about Jessie's burritos wrapped in silver aluminum foil.

"Hey, shut up man," Jessie barked.

"But I have homemade tortillas," Ernie broadcast.

As I readjusted my cube of bread, it occurred to me that I had never eaten a homemade tortilla.

By the time I was ready for our hike, so was the troop. I looked up just as Juan barked, "March."

We hesitated, having never before done this. Then a few feet stepped forward, and we stumbled into each other with yells of "Watch out, man" and Spanish swear words. To an outside observer, we didn't march, we agitated.

Actually, it was very difficult to coordinate our steps because of the ice chests. I suppose they were simply copying their older brothers or cousins, but the Hispanic kids didn't have backpacks and instead just loaded what they needed (mainly food and six-packs of bottles filled with soda) into two pairs of metal ice chests, slightly dented but functional.

They had paired up and were trying to march with the chest held between them, each lugging a side and the metal handles cutting into hands and fingers. After a few steps, some of them took off the bandannas from their necks and wrapped them around their hands to cushion the handles. The chests were really portable iceboxes and they looked heavy, real heavy. You could see a trail of melted ice dripping from the bottom and soon the cases were being dragged more than carried.

Remember later, Bob, when we got the bright idea to lighten the load and fling the blocks of ice? We all watched as the white ice sailed in the air before landing with a thud and rolling in the dirt and weeds. The ice immediately began to melt in the warm spring sun, and I wondered what the following troops thought when they found a miniature iceberg in the middle of a dusty field?

The stuff that didn't fit in the chests was put into

brown paper bags and handed to the younger guys. Tommy proudly walked with his clothes and blanket in a little suitcase in one hand, the other clutching a paper bag that was slowly getting crushed with each step.

But we were all aided in our march by the record player Valente had brought. He carried a plastic, portable, battery-powered little machine that played 45s. Cradling the player with both hands (a buddy, Lalo, carried the stack of 45s), Val tried to keep the player level so it wouldn't skip whenever he stepped over a hole or rock.

He set our pace to the tune of "Louie, Louie" echoing over the open fields. Later, when we began to fatigue and the ice chests were dragging, Val switched songs to "La Bamba" and renewed our spirits.

The Del Rey Boy Scout troop had arrived, behind the Scouts from Fresno and neighboring communities. We walked just the way we were.

Your Scouting buddy,
Mas

Flowers for Soldiers

Dear Uncle George,

Every Memorial Day, our family would visit the cemetery where you are buried. We'd prepare two bouquets of flowers, rolling them in newspaper for the car trip. We set them in a glass quart jar, wrapped with aluminum foil on the outside so they'd look nice.

My job was to help with transportation. I would sit in the back seat of the car, balancing a jar between my five-year-old feet, one bouquet between my knees while my sister or brother did the same with the other. We tolerated the twenty-minute drive from the farm to the cemetery as water splashed out of the jars and onto our socks.

At the cemetery we parked and carried the flowers to your grave and Grandpa's grave, only a few yards apart. Grandma leaned over, cleaned off her husband's headstone, set down the flowers and silently bowed. She repeated the process at your grave, pausing to remember her firstborn. Dad and mom followed, then us kids. We could tell if the other aunts and uncles had already visited and left their flowers before us. Looking up, we saw dozens of other families had joined us, repeating the ritual with their loved ones.

No one was in a rush, so often I had a chance to wander around, recognizing names near Grandpa's headstone, counting the numerous Japanese family names at the Selma cemetery. Grandma wandered too, hands clasped behind her, quietly walking and visiting a family friend who had passed away, whispering to herself. Mom would walk, stopping to set upright a jar with flowers that had toppled over in a gust of wind. Dad seemed to pause at your grave, never saying anything, reading the stone of his lost older brother.

GEORGE H. MASUMOTO
PFC 442 INF
WORLD WAR II
JUNE 4, 1919
OCT. 16, 1944

I looked for names of other soldiers, wondering if you knew them. Did you fight side by side with anyone, and die together? Unless they were Japanese Americans, I doubt you knew the others.

During World War II, even though our nation fought a common enemy, we were still a land of racial segregation in the military. I remember reading about a group of African Americans overcoming obstacles to form the Tuskegee Airmen, America's first black military air corps of pilots and ground support units.

You probably never heard of them but I believe you understood their struggle.

Uncle, you were part of another division. Prior to December 7, 1941, you had been drafted into the U.S. Army. After the bombing of Pearl Harbor and declaration of war against Japan, Japanese Americans like our family were suddenly labeled the enemy. Even though you were born in California and an American citizen, your loyalty was questioned. The Army took away your gun and weapons, so how could you continue your training? The government imprisoned your parents and siblings, locking them in relocation camps, yet you fought for freedom. You joined the 442nd Regimental Combat Team, an all–Japanese American fighting division, and proved your loyalty, tragically falling to honest German bullets that didn't care what you looked like, the color of your skin, and what country your parents immigrated from.

Now, every Memorial Day, I think about you and soldiers. You died for something clear at the time. But now it's growing harder and harder to remember all the reasons why soldiers battle. Making war may not be so simple anymore. Today, another generation sacrifices and a question arises: why do we fight?

I don't know, it's too big of a question for me. I do believe the truth lies in something much simpler. Your fighting and dying changed our family history. My grandparents lost their eldest child, the number one son in the family. My father, uncles, and aunts lost a brother, the older brother who was supposed to help the family plant roots in American soil.

Did you fight for our country? Did you die for our family? Did the contradictions, confusion, and fear challenge you? I believe the answer to all was yes, equally yes. The patriotism inherent in the first question did not necessarily overshadow the pain of the second question, and the internal struggle of the last one.

I believe in the fog of war: the issues, causes, and justifications for fighting are usually not that clear. We may want absolutes to help clarify our reasoning, but wars carry multiple meanings and many perspectives.

Years later, your mother, my grandmother, grew flowers specifically for Memorial Day. She tended them throughout the year, ultimately carefully wrapping them for a cemetery visit, carrying them to her family's graves. The contrast between the headstones jolts my thinking.

One is my grandfather's, your father, an Issei (first-generation immigrant from Japan) who could never own land in America because he was classified as an "Oriental foreigner." He must have been crushed by the World War II upheaval of relocation. His American dream shattered, he became an old, obsolete man, stripped of everything.

The other is yours, the grave of the uncle I never met. You were the first child of our family born in America. I believe you carried an immigrant family's promise of hope in a new land. Yet I only know you by a black-and-white photograph of a soldier in an Army uniform. And the stories that were never to be.

Every Memorial Day, despite the late spring weather and warm temperatures, a fog creeps into my mind and never adds clarity. However, it continues to create the memory of a soldier.

Uncle, I will remember you.

Your nephew,
Mas

I Remember Winter

Dear Nikiko and Korio,

   Children, I do a lot of thinking in winter. The days are short, the nights long. It's a good time to ponder and reflect—an art form disappearing in our high-tech, fast-paced world. But the fog, coupled with getting older, makes me remember.

   I remember the first time eating fresh peaches in December, imported from Chile, and thinking, "This is crazy, it's winter."

   I remember listening to the sound of dew dripping from the leaves as the morning frost melts.

   I remember when I couldn't wait until Christmas day.

   I remember that every December 7th my family could feel the ghosts of World War II and the internment of Japanese Americans. Some people used to blame my family for the bombs falling at Pearl Harbor.

   I remember spinning in a car on black ice.

   I remember standing on our farmhouse porch in heavy fog as it rolled in around me. I felt like I was on a ship at sea, moving through the dark waters, terrified by the loss of sight, thrilled by the adventures ahead.

I remember the aroma of baked goods in the kitchen when it got cold outside. It felt warm inside, like home.

I remember studying the Sears Catalogue as our wish book for gifts.

I remember waiting in holiday traffic to turn left on Shaw Avenue and it taking five light rotations.

I remember when it snowed in Fresno in the 1960s. We made snowmen and had snowball fights. No one drove anywhere that day—we were not used to the white stuff on the ground.

I remember pruning and tying vines in the damp cold and a cane slipping loose and slapping my cheek. It stung and my eyes watered. Once I even cried, but I simply moved on to the next vine.

I remember wearing the same Christmas sweater to my in-laws' for about ten years. When else *can* you wear red and green and look like an elf?

I remember trying to watch a high school football game in the fog. You could only guess what happened.

I remember gifts of dried fruit that old folks loved. As I get older, I understand why.

I remember my first kiss at a Christmas Ball. It was warm and wet, and I still smile.

I remember eating fresh, ice-cold oranges just picked from the tree.

I remember the '91 freeze: water pipes cracked, oranges froze, and it never got warmer than 28 degrees for days.

I remember my elementary school friends leaving every winter to return to Mexico. They came back in the spring. School was hard for them.

I remember a school treat of a bag of Christmas candy and an orange or apple. These stories only age me even more in your eyes.

I remember the silence of a foggy winter day. The only sounds I heard were my pruning shears snipping and clipping, or my own breathing.

I remember learning how mild our Central Valley winters are after listening to your mother's Wisconsin family. One Christmas day, their living room fish tank froze. The fish were still alive, but "moving real slow."

I remember driving in awe at the sparkle of lights down Christmas Tree Lane.

I remember our milkman Rudy's truck breaking down one cold day. We invited him in for coffee.

I remember visiting Yosemite in winter and taking one of the quietest walks in my life.

I remember when our Buddhist youth group sold Christmas cards as a fund-raiser.

I remember worrying, when it rained on an "electric Holiday parade," that the two elements didn't mix.

I remember making Japanese *mochi* to welcome the new year. Extended families got together to pound sweet rice and make little cakes of sticky, gooey, and dense dough.

I remember the flavors of fresh tamales near the holidays and wishing we were Mexican.

I remember eating black-eyed peas for New Year's luck.

I remember returning from an elementary school basketball tournament when it was so foggy that our coach had us run in front of the car so he could keep it on the road. Crazy. Dangerous. But we thought it was fun.

I remember when no holiday ads appeared before Thanksgiving and the day after Christmas didn't mean shopping.

I remember making out with a girl I barely knew to celebrate the new year. Today I struggle to stay awake that late.

I remember running into a young friend who had just returned from deer hunting. In her camouflages and embarrassed by her appearance, she still was proud of shooting her first deer. It was a rite of passage.

I remember driving into the foggy valley down the Grapevine south of Bakersfield. It was like descending into a giant, fluffy pillow.

I remember, in the third grade, realizing that not all kids got Christmas presents. It was the first time I had witnessed poverty.

I remember my senior year in high school and realizing that after winter break my grades wouldn't affect my college application.

I remember our first artificial Christmas tree, with shiny aluminum "branches." Dad said it would last a lifetime. We still have it, but don't use it.

I remember celebrating the shortest day of the year, December 21st (some years the 22nd), and knowing every day would start getting longer.

I remember the holiday window display at Hanford Furniture.

I remember still believing in Santa until I was old. Wonderfully, you children did the same.

I remember coming in from the fields by five p.m. because it was so dark, and not feeling guilty about cutting my workday short.

I remember watching countless small-town holiday parades. Each community felt its parade was the Valley's best.

I remember cross-country skiing and snow camping in the Sierras, and making a small shelter out of snow. It was one of the coldest nights in my life.

I remember watching JFK being inaugurated in the bitter, bitter cold.

I remember, as an eighth grader, playing in our country school's holiday program. We actually had a small orchestra (with three violins and a cello—I played French horn). We were just awful, but our patient music teacher still loved us.

I remember going to the Cal Bowl in Fresno.

I remember when, as a kid, my brother got a pink shirt for a Christmas present. I laughed loud and long at him, only to open my gift and find a pink shirt, too.

I remember working in the fog and hearing a distant dog barking, a neighbor's tractor engine churn and the hum of machinery miles away. Sounds carry differently in the fog.

I remember watching kids from affluent areas giving gifts to poor kids, and how sadly awkward it felt.

I remember becoming melancholy, usually in December, while looking back over the past year: What had I really accomplished? What good did I do?

Fondly,
Your dad

P.S. What's your favorite "I remember winter" memory? Send them to me at masumoto@aol.com.

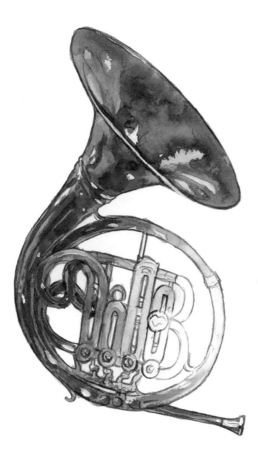

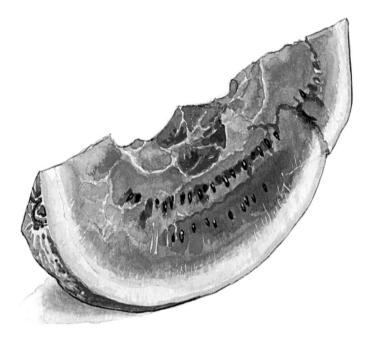

I Remember Summer

Dear Niki and Kori,

I want to pass on to you, my children, remembrances of summers past. These memories make me sound old, but they give character to this place we call home and attach significance to everyday events—at least to me. In my memories, the ordinary becomes extraordinary. This isn't objective journalism; I'm not reporting the facts and instead am offering insight into how things connect for me. I want to share my emotions and the elation of summer memories.

I remember one July when it was so hot in the fields that all my work clothes were soaked with sweat, from the headband of my hat to my work shirt, jeans, shorts, and socks. Even my leather work boots and belt were wet and dark. Only the belt loops on my pants were not stained with sweat. Now that's hot.

I remember as a kid eating a juicy peach I had spied and watched ripen for weeks. It burst with juice and the explosion of flavor was so amazing I was shocked. The taste stayed with me as the nectar trickled down my face and dripped onto my white t-shirt, and I would be cursed forever trying to rediscover that perfect peach.

I remember my first Dodger game and buying a baseball autographed by all the players and coaches, including Koufax, Drysdale, Durocher, and Hodges. I particularly liked Wally Moon's signature.

I remember green, bulbous tomato hornworms and my grandmother squishing them in her fist.

I remember our farm dogs panting in the heat. One trusty old dog, appropriately named Dusty, had medium-length fur but suffered in the heat because I never, that I can remember, brushed her. (She was, after all, a farm dog.) The dog days of summer meant her thick red tongue would hang out of her mouth, almost touching the ground as she lay in the shade of a grapevine. I tried to mimic her panting to keep cool, too, taking short and quick breaths. It only tired me even more and I just couldn't get Dusty's calm look on my face: her eyes half closed, softly panting, and a very relaxed, drooping tongue.

I remember eating the coldest watermelon, chilled by blocks of ice in a galvanized metal tub. We gorged ourselves and spit the seeds at each other.

I remember going to a Buddhist Obon, a Japanese American dance festival in the streets around the church in West Fresno. We bought snow cones and played bingo and carnival games. The dancers, dressed in colorful costumes, whirled to the Japanese music echoing over the streets. I watched my *baachan* (grandmother), who had emigrated from Japan in 1918. Squatting on the sidewalk, watching the festivities, I think she returned for a moment to her homeland and the village she thought she'd never see again. Later that month, I also remember a "Jamaica" festival in Del Rey. Peeking through the wooden fence, I watched the dancers swinging to the loud and romantic Mexican music. Perhaps these farmworkers also returned to a homeland with each song.

I remember tubing the Kings River, a slow and simple ride with friends—a Sanger tradition.

I remember our '58 Ford Fairlane with a huge V-8 engine (gas was only twenty-five cents a gallon) and big fins. We rode around the countryside a few long summer evenings with the windows wide open and feeling lucky. A sign of good times: sleek, modern, and the future could only be bigger (and presumably better).

I remember swamp coolers blowing wet air into our house. We kids squeezed in front to cool off, and I can picture my dad in the evening, after a long day in the fields, standing in front without a t-shirt, with his eyes closed, enjoying a moment of decadence.

I remember helping coach my wife's softball team, which wasn't very good. One summer evening, playing a much better team, they took the field and it took forever to get the other team out. In fact, before the first out, a house caught fire in the neighborhood behind center field. From the dugout, I watched the smoke then flames dance on the roof while the game continued. Firefighters tried to put out the inferno, but the house burned to the ground—all before the third out of the inning was made and her team mercifully got to come in from the field.

I remember camping in the peach orchards with my brother. We drew no lines between our fields of work and fields of play.

I remember trying to fry an egg on the road; my brother and I cracked it and watched it sit there, doing nothing, until a car approached.

I remember playing outside with my cousins until nine or ten o'clock at night.

I remember Fourth of July parties we hosted on the farm. The Picolo Petes drove the dogs crazy and the black snakes scattered in the yard. Usually, someone got burned holding a sparkler. Later, as adults, we made flying flowers out of spinning fireworks and once, when an idiotic, rich relative came from the city, we convinced him to hold a "Roman Candle" sparkling fountain over his head like the Statue of Liberty. Someone stopped him before his hair caught fire.

I remember one Fourth of July party when the heat was at least 105 degrees. We sweated a lot but still enjoyed ourselves and, as people were leaving, someone noticed a friend had brought a sweater. When asked, she explained that sometimes, at night, it gets cold out in the country. (She was from the city of Easton.)

I remember that as a treat and break from the summer harvest, Dad would load us in the car for a trip to a drive-in hamburger place in town. Dad liked Norm's or Lesterburger. I can still remember local TV celebrity Al Radka and his advertisements. He'd point to the lettuce in a burger and ask, "Say, what's that? Lettuce? Lettuce? Well, let us eat it." Then he took a huge bite. It was stupid, but it is stuck in my memory.

I remember celebrating the last day of school listening

to Alice Cooper's "School's Out for Summer," and it then taking only about three days before I got bored.

I remember swimming in an irrigation canal with my pal Bob. The water was so cold it hurt. Then we got to thinking about where the water had come from upstream and the times we threw stuff in the ditch or peed in the current. We jumped out and decided we really didn't want to swim.

I remember Playland at Roeding Park. Riding the roller coaster was a thrill and the merry-go-round fun. It wasn't quite like Disneyland, but the cotton candy tasted the same and you could go anywhere on the paddleboats. I'd watch families and couples enjoy each other on a weekend outing and think, "This is what city parks are supposed to be about."

I remember making out in a car with a girlfriend. A hot summer night literally meant that when it was 90 degrees at eleven p.m., it was destined to be a hot summer night. We only kissed. Really, that's it.

I remember the ice cream on a scorching summer day at the Hanford Superior Dairy. Walking in was like a step into the past, a scene out of "Happy Days." I learned to eat the treat slowly, using my spoon to sculpt the ice cream, shaving off small spoonfuls from the outside edges and savoring each bite; little by little, lingering as long as we could inside.

I remember standing with friends in the middle of a fig orchard north of Fresno during a summer night: stillness, silence, darkness. Only on the horizon was the glow of city lights. We were frozen in time, and little did any of us know the city would march out there within a few decades.

Fondly,
Your dad

P.S. What's your favorite "I remember summer" memory? Send them to me at masumoto@aol.com.

Out on the Porch

Dear Nikiko and Korio,

Although you kids only knew of the most recent vintage, our farmhouse had three different porches. The original one faced east, a small landing for a small home. I can imagine someone riding up on a horse, jumping off and, as the animal grazed on the grasses under a yard tree, neighbors visiting.

In the 1950s, our home was remodeled and the front porch opened to the south. But something happened about that time: air conditioning. People began to hunker down indoors and porches were quickly forgotten. (Soon to follow was the birth of attached garages, and suburbs; houses, yards, and neighborhoods designed to keep others out and homeowners shut in.)

Air conditioning was a status symbol; people with money could stay inside during our valley's hot summer months while poor folks had to endure the elements. Staying inside implied being clean; outside, you sweated and became dirty. Porches symbolized the old days, a lack of affluence, a relic of the Great Depression. (I read a similar story about the Midwest, the arrival of electricity and jello. City folks were the first to have the benefits of electricity to power such things as refrigerators. That meant the "poor" country folks couldn't bring jello to the church potlucks.)

You children grew up on our present porch. After coming back to the farm and moving into this house twenty-five years ago, your mom and I quickly discerned that we needed a real farmhouse porch with a wide veranda and white rails. Now our porch runs along most of the southern exposure. Its redwood planks remain straight and aged; the steps are beginning to show wear and now have character; and the rails have three coats of paint.

Over the years, you kids took over the deck and considered it a huge playpen. We took an obligatory photograph as you walked out onto the porch and left home on the first day of each school year.

The porch was big enough to play soccer on, set up tables of food for family reunions, or entertain a gallery of friends as they watched Fourth of July fireworks. Our porch was an extension of our home.

On the porch we've hosted book parties and family gatherings, setting up a long table where all the guests could sit. Once, with a buddy, we shared a summer evening with fine cigars; something, Korio, you won't let me forget. It bothered you to see your father smoking on your porch (even if only once a year).

From the porch you kids witnessed the violent June 1995 hailstorm that devastated our peaches. Another time you saw me collapse on the deck from the summer heat and whisper, "This farm is gonna kill me." From it, we continue to share the annual rite of spring, witnessing the pale green of young vine shoots reaching for the sky, full of promise. Our family's work is never hidden from view out on the porch.

We share the space with pets, spiders, lizards, and who knows what else lurking beneath the wooden planks. And aren't all porches supposed to have wicker chairs? The kind that cats claim as their thrones or dogs love to lie next to, both creatures curled in a harmony you wish the entire world shared.

We all slow down on the porch. I rest on a simple wooden bench, just the right height for a short person to sit down and take refuge from farm work. Not a place to hide but to pause; I have to think twice before standing up again. People today seem to take comfort in escaping into their homes. Armed with technology and big screen TVs, home movie-theater sound systems, and virtual vacations on computers, they disconnect. From my bench, I have a gentle reminder of the world that awaits me out in the fields. But perhaps not just right now. I savor the moment with a cool drink in the late spring or summer, finding the right excuse to rest: "I have plenty of work time, it doesn't get dark until late."

From this vantage point, I can scan the farm and survey the world. In the evening I can hear baby barn owls screeching for food and the sound of the adults taking flight: whoosh, whoosh, whoosh. I look up and see the ghost of their faces in the moonlight. I watch the fog slip by on a cold winter day and feel as if we're on a ship cutting through the moisture, moving through time. During harvest, I can see our orchards and vineyards, hear water splashing out of irrigation valves, and imagine the trees getting a cool drink as the heat ripens fruit. The farm is never far from us and our porch gives me a sense of place.

On the porch we're half inside and half outside; away from the daily physical struggle of farm work, but not yet distracted by phone calls or e-mails. It's a place of transition between public and private spaces, preparing to venture out into the world or taking shelter in our home.

Children, you don't know this, but my favorite times of the day are either the early morning when the world is just awakening or the middle of the night when I imagine everyone except me is asleep. I'll stand out on the porch and lean against the rail. It takes a minute before the quiet is heard and all seems well. Then I'm renewed for the day.

Our porch is where you kids can watch me grow old. I'll age with the wood, wear down like the footpath marking our daily trail from the steps to the front door. I, too, will have scars and wear the weathered signs of the seasons.

Tales were told and retold out on our porch, growing with generations. Old folks need a place where their stories can be shared, a place with memories and stories we leave behind.

I think we should have a Valley porch day: tell stories as we all take to our porches, wave to each other like a scene from the past, and celebrate who we are. We're more porch people here than big-city folk, and our architecture needs to mirror us.

Kids, take our porch with you, wherever you go, to the places you will grow to call home.

Love,
Dad

PART TWO

Farming Food

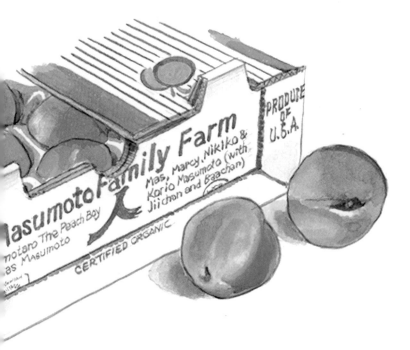

Eating Rejects

Dear Alice,

I have a confession that you, the chef who launched "California Cuisine" from her Berkeley restaurant, Chez Panisse, might enjoy: I grew up eating rejects.

On our eighty-acre family farm near Fresno, California, we raised peaches, nectarines, and raisins. Mom and Dad worked the fields, three kids helped out when we could, and our summers were devoted to the home packing shed. We harvested from June to September. A work crew picked the fruit and in the shed we sorted and packed them into boxes, ready for shipment to grocery stores.

The peach culls interested me the most. Some were cut or bruised and insects damaged a few, which terrified Dad. (He believed in that old joke: when you eat a peach, what's worse than finding a worm? Answer: half a worm.) Other culled fruit had aptly named defects: "split pits," "suture cracks," or "misshapen."

Dad hated the green fruit the most because we couldn't pack them. The phrase "could have been" accompanied each one, the idea of lost potential bothered us all.

But most of all, I loved the soft, overripe, gushy ones.

First, the aroma grabbed my attention: these smelled like real peaches. Biting into one, the juices would drip down my cheeks and dangle on my chin. Then, the nectar exploded in my mouth as the pulp slid past the tongue and down the throat. I stopped and savored the moment of pleasure: smacking my lips, sucking my tongue, and still tasting peach. I gorged myself and grew fat.

I was spoiled: I ate the best and expected the best. Yet I was confused: why couldn't we sell these gems? Dad explained that the fruit would start rotting or "breaking down" as soon as we put them in the box. Once, he brought home a rejected carton with juice dripping from the bottom. It never made it to market.

Dad understood flavors as well as the realities of marketplace. We set a goal of doing our best and trusted that the old peach varieties would keep ripening after we picked them. If they were good when we packed them, they could become great in transit. But I still savored the rewards for being part of a peach farm. I knew the rejects were often the best.

After college, I came back to the farm and got married. Marcy's and my dream was to provide learning experiences for our children.

When our daughter, Nikiko, was thirteen years old, we treated ourselves to a journey: we followed our peaches to market. Every summer, the family packed specialty boxes for select buyers, usually restaurants or gourmet retailers specializing in organic produce. We tried to make these our best (although Nikiko also knew of the "other" best ones, the gushy culls we ate in the shed).

Yet Nikiko was confused as to why I was so fanatical about culling out those that weren't quite ripe or had some minor flaw. I was terrified not by the cosmetic defects but rather by the maturity of each peach: I dreamed of perfection. Nikiko blankly stared back as I attempted to expound about the art of growing peaches. I failed in my explanations, my words too abstract, my metaphors confusing.

That summer, we journeyed from our farm in Fresno to the San Francisco Bay Area for a quick trip in the middle of harvest, a rare event for the farmer to pull himself away from his fields. While there, we visited your restaurant in Berkeley. Alice, you had been using our fruits for years. We were honored to be part of your delicious revolution—to eat foods in season and grown locally.

At the restaurant, they were preparing our peaches for dinner desserts. Nikiko saw something I could never convey. Each peach was washed and carefully placed in the middle of a white plate, stem side down. Later, just before serving, they'd add a quick drizzle of color, like a raspberry swirl. Nikiko's peach stood alone, as the centerpiece. She stared at the trays and smiled; I sensed a type of closure. She now understood how the peaches were served, eaten, and hopefully enjoyed. She learned of perfection only by knowing the rejects.

Our second child was a son named Korio who was much more relaxed while growing up, as were his parents. He, too, spent summers in the packing shed and worked hard, though he'd rather play. He delighted in our annual summer ritual—with each different variety of peach or nectarine, I'd find the first ripe piece of fruit from the orchard and share it with the family.

We'd stand around the butcher block island in the kitchen, taking a thin slice of the latest treasure and grinning when it melted in our mouths. I wanted to teach a sense of value to the kids: as we all did our best and if nature cooperated, we just might, with luck, get close to perfection.

There were contradictions, I tried to explain, such as growing something that may be getting so expensive our friends couldn't afford them. But value was all relative and personal. This was much too complex for the then ten-year-old Korio, so he simply asked for another slice.

I decided to show a real-life example of value to him, so we visited a local grocery store. I explained that the price of our organic fruit—which may sell for three dollars a pound—was actually not that expensive. First, I hoped people ate all of the fruit because it was ripe and didn't waste half and toss it away. Second, you had to compare prices relative to each other. So I selected Twinkies as an example. The three-ounce sugary sweet treat sold for about a dollar. I calculated that to be over five dollars a pound and told my son, "See, now which is more expensive?"

He carefully eyed the sponge cake with cream filling, then looked at his father and nodded. I felt proud, having taught a lesson about values—both in our work as a family farm and the real price of foods we eat. I turned to walk out but was interrupted.

"But Dad," Korio pleaded, pointing to the packages of Twinkies. "Aren't we going to continue the research and buy some to take home?"

I felt rejected. All I could do was weakly smile.

Food lessons will always be with us, part of our continuing education, right Alice?

Thanks,
Mas

Mr. Johnson's Curse

Dear Mr. Johnson,

What were you thinking when you planted a lush-growing sorghum plant on your Alabama plantation in 1843? Little did you realize your innovation would spread throughout the nation, forever attaching your name to one of the most noxious and hideous weeds. Farmers and gardeners curse you when this weed infests a vegetable plot, row crop, vineyard, or orchard: "Damned Johnson grass!"

You thought the seeds from either Africa or the Middle East would grow to become feed for your cattle, the perfect ground cover for your lands, a high-producing and desirable perennial grass. How could you have known that the normally palatable forage becomes poisonous to livestock if its normal growth is interrupted by drought or frost? You couldn't measure the toxic accumulation of hydrocyanic acid in the surviving roots. You had the image of a nice patch of tall grass gracefully growing and swaying in the wind.

What were you, nuts?

Hadn't you heard that Governor Means of South Carolina had already experimented with this monster a decade earlier? He had written, "The big grass inspired terror and no one will look at my place." He could not sell his plantation infected with this weed. I thought all you plantation owners ran in the same circles.

But no, you were then called "Colonel Johnson" and with a Southerner's arrogance, you probably thought you could do as you pleased with your property. So you sowed the fertile bottomlands of the Alabama River and became part of history. With the Civil War, cavalry horses simply ate the lush grasses and spread the seeds throughout the south. Then later, in the late 1800s, your seeds could easily contaminate a nation as members of Congress passed out hundreds of thousands of free seed samples annually or when the United States Department of Agriculture distributed more than one million seed samples per year.

Was this your revenge for losing the war? A single plant can produce over five thousand seeds and lie dormant in the ground for twenty years. Chop the stalks and new shoots push up from the earth with more vigor. Burn the plant and it seems to thrive on cleansing, easily out-competing anything else with regrowth.

The plant's secret weapon: the underground stems called rhizomes. From each segment of root, new shoots rise like a head of the Greek mythic Hydra. Cut off the head and two will appear. Slice the rhizomes into small pieces and each will regenerate its own plant. Disking and cultivating the ground spreads them even more, the plant delightedly invading any disturbed ground.

The plant grows dense, up to eight feet tall, easily monopolizing sunlight and crowding out any other growth. Try to shovel the roots and your blade will strike a contorted root mass of thick rhizomes often tangled in a massive underground ball. Miss some roots and they will start producing a natural toxin, preventing other plants from growing close to them. Your grass, Mister Johnson, does not make for a good neighbor.

How foolish you and others were, thinking you could control the forces of nature, import something for your own use, believing only good would come from the innocent-looking reddish seeds. Your goal, of course, was simply to produce more and more—stories of this grass generating over two tons of forage with each cutting danced in your head. This was America, land of new opportunities with unbound fortunes for those with an enterprising will. Instead, you cursed a nation.

Some have claimed your grass is not that bad, were it not so aggressive. Swine apparently relish the roots, which can be quite palatable. Cut for hay, it becomes nutritious (so long as the plant is not stressed into producing natural toxins). Some seed dealers actually sell the seeds. I certainly would not call them my friends.

While yanking out your grass from my vineyard, many times I have slit my fingers. The razor-sharp leaves slice unprotected hands. My grandmother called your weed *abunai kusa* (dangerous grass). She was correct; unchecked it will strangle a farm and the farmer, stealing water from trees, shading grapes from the sun, overpowering a vineyard, and striking terror in a harvest worker.

An invasive weed—that's an understatement. I've woken up in the middle of my sleep from a nightmare of Johnson grass sweeping across our valley, marching like an army, destroying acres and acres of land. In my dream I see men and women waging war, cutting down stalks, never allowing green growth to survive. But the roots lie quiet in the earth, waiting for exhaustion and resprouting with vengeance.

Your legacy has bankrupted scores of farmers. I've heard stories of range wars, neighbor pitted against neighbor, your seeds of destruction carried in the bowels of cattle. One story ended with a bitter divorce; a son-in-law could never understand why his father-in-law hated him. Apparently, someone had to be blamed when your grass became established on his ranch.

I do have a conspiracy theory: the Johnson family had a patent on the French plow, a complicated piece of equipment that will reach under a grapevine and scoop out a mass of earth and, hopefully, Johnson grass plants and most of their roots. The tool does well but is not perfect against this perfect enemy.

Or perhaps your family had envisioned future shares in Monsanto, the company that invented Roundup. The herbicide is absorbed into the plant and will kill most of it. With heavy infestations, you have to reapply the chemical to kill all the rhizomes.

(But like your folly, today some scientists have experimented with plant genes, making some crops resistant to Roundup. Monsanto's hope was to patent farm crops that could be sprayed with Roundup to kill weeds such as Johnson grass and thereby destroy evil. Already, after only a few years, nature has found a way to survive. Some weeds, like mare's tail, are now growing resistant to Roundup.)

Mister Johnson, you have taught me one lesson. I am humbled. Your grass, an alien species, invaded our nation and planted roots. A plague? No, that would imply a cure. A curse. Yes, something we must learn to live with. I will accept Johnson's curse but will continue to engage in battle on my organic farm. You have left your imprint and I do often speak your name, accompanied occasionally by profanity.

With disdain,
Mas Masumoto

Humbling

Dear Kopi, Jason, Kevin, and Angelo,

Weathermen and weatherwomen share something with farmers: the nightly forecast.

Throughout September and October, I listened to your every word as fifty tons of raisins sat exposed in my vineyard. I worried when you spoke of a rain, trying to decipher the difference between "slight" versus "good chance." I learned of virga, rain that doesn't reach the ground, and I followed Doppler images of a storm front sliding across our state. I watched selfishly with glee as a low-pressure zone slipped down the coast in mid-October, bypassing us and parking to the west of Los Angeles, then pounding Southern California with floods.

I understand percentages with rain. First, 50 percent means that one out of two times you predict rain, it will (or won't). And second, when we're talking about measurable rain, .15 or one-half inch mean the same. But when you casually mentioned "pack your umbrella," my heart raced.

Farmers are in the business of predicting the future. You anticipate the weather, and I live with each projection: changing my work; sometimes spending hundreds or thousands of dollars in a preemptive strike; applying water to my vines before the spring freeze; rushing to harvest ripening fruit in advance of a summer heat wave; or hiring workers to roll up raisin trays when rain threatens in the fall.

Yet we live with the past, often speaking in terms of averages, records, and of course, disasters. I vividly remember the devastating freeze of 1991 and a freak June hailstorm in 1995. Certainly we recall the wave after wave of late October rains in 2004 (when many predicted a 20 percent chance of rain) and the blistering heat during this past July and August, when thirty of thirty-one days soared over 100 degrees on our valley floor. While others quickly forget, farmers and weather people remember.

Still, my aging memory lies when you speak of averages. Weather statistics are calculated with data from only the past thirty years. It may well have been "hotter when I was a kid," but those years are not part of current averages. My childhood no longer counts, which makes me feel old, very old.

We work with an inexact science and cannot project with high confidence. How long into the future are forecasts accurate? A week, a few days, a couple of hours? Computer models crunch the numbers and base predictions on projections: they really are just alternative opinions and no one really knows.

Increasingly, in a world dominated by technology, systems seem to function as if they can control the weather. Heat can be overcome by air conditioning, storm run-offs avoided by constructing higher barriers, and raindrops dodged by erecting tents and larger arenas. Even some farmers claim to evade hail by shooting cannons of air (and noise) at thunderheads as they are forming. As a result, we blindly venture into places with historic risk and attitudes that we can "ride out" storms and conquer nature. The public lives with a rhythm oblivious to weather. People expect packages delivered, products to arrive at market, and schedules to be kept no matter the weather. Ask when the last time was that weather was included in a business plan.

But winters are supposed to be cold and summers hot, and hurricanes and other severe storms come with lots of wind and rain. Yet homes are built on flood plains, ignoring the experience of generations before who avoided certain places because they were at the mercy of nature. Recent hurricanes, Katrina and Rita, exposed the delicate underbelly of our thinking: we don't control weather, we cannot determine our destiny with nature, we can't always do what we please. Those who continue to believe they can weather any storm have lost respect for the elements and a sense of who they are: they have forgotten humility.

Few professions must learn to live with nature. Most businesses are too protected and the public too insulated from weather. The typical response to weather crises is to build something higher and stronger or to battle the elements by buying a bigger machine that's faster with more power. People believe they can outrun a storm or wait out a hurricane.

Weather forecasters and farmers don't fit this modern thinking. We're "old school" and have been taught about forces out of our control. Your reputations are on the line, my livelihood at risk. We have learned you don't mess with mother.

But being humbled before nature creates a rhythm we're not used to. It's slow—a slow assessment of damage, the slow process of rebuilding, even the slow healing.

In the end, what we take away from nature and her cycles of weather are stories: memories of a killer freeze, the perfect storm, or a devastating summer drought; human tales of survival and the will to move forward. Or an epiphany: to give thanks for what we have. Maybe, just maybe, all that material stuff we have really doesn't matter.

Recent Gulf Coast hurricanes exposed the folly of trying to downplay the wrath and unpredictability of nature. Katrina showed the world how under-prepared people and our government were. Rita tricked expert news teams who were racing to find the right camera angle in Galveston, Texas, to cover the devastation, only to discover at the last minute that the storm had swerved to the east. The best reporting let those people impacted simply tell their stories.

We are not in control of nature and our psyche needs to rediscover that. We may have too much technology. Was my watching a potential raisin-threatening storm on satellite imagery any different from my dad watching the western skies, licking a finger, and holding it up to sense the change in wind currents? In either case, all a farmer could do was sit and wait.

Where we try to impose our will on the landscape, nature sometimes snaps back. Perhaps the best we can hope for is to cohabitate with her and accept the realities of weather. I predict that all of us, at some point in our lifetime, will be humbled by nature. Weather people and farmers are in the front row for this wild ride every year. With every clear and sunny prediction, a storm continues to brew, somewhere off on the horizon.

Sincerely,
Mas

Art of Optimism

Dear Jim,

As a journalist, you questioned my optimism: "In the face of the multitude of problems facing our valley and especially family farms, how can you stay so optimistic?"

Because I don't know any better.

Farmers suffer from a terminal optimism: the weather will be good, the crops should be about right, the prices could be fair. We're at the mercy of forces out of our control and perhaps we gain optimism from our smallness and lack of power. We have learned to trust that things will somehow work out.

I recall hearing stories about those who survived the savage economic depression of the 1930s. For many, blind optimism kept them going, clinging to a belief that things would get better. Hope was the last to die. Perhaps that should be my maxim.

An old farmer once told me a story about the label mounted on his peach boxes. His label read "Yamamoto and Sons," which struck me as odd, since he only had one son. (I promised to change his family name should I ever publicly share this story.) His reply, "Shucks, I made that label even before I had kids. I was just being a good, optimistic farmer."

Farmers have perfected the art of optimism: we hope for mild winters with oranges, weather in September that can be trusted for raisins, and hailstorms to fall innocently in open fields and avoid peaches and nectarines. Naively, we translate our thinking into action: planning for nice wet winters and dry springs, anticipating the escape of summer heat waves, looking forward to the arrival of fall so we can start all over. We'd be great fans of the Chicago Cubs or Boston Red Sox. I once saw on TV a sign someone had raised after his lovable Cubs lost the opening day game: "Wait till next year." The slogan of optimism for our valley?

But today, some of the best farmers are beginning to learn the spirit of the land is based not on control but cooperation. They seek a sustainable balance in their work, using natural farming methods—biological controls, providing habitat for beneficial insects, and a reduction of toxic pesticides. Much of this relies on nature to slowly take care of things—if not now, perhaps next season; a perspective of trust in contrast to the controlling dominance of industrial factory farming. A "wait till next year" perspective is built on a foundation of trust.

Jim, I believe this agrarian-based optimism permeates the culture of this valley, including its cities. Recent polls from the Public Policy Institute seem to verify this: people are very positive about living here. It's part of my "good enough theory" about Valley life: We tolerate poverty, inequality, and shortcomings but remain content. Some will claim our valley is becoming a Mecca for lousy jobs. But it's still a job. How can we be happy when, for some, times are so bad? Naiveté or ignorance or optimism—a perception of a cup half-full.

I find an odd blend of an American independent spirit in these lands: Love it or leave it. Since more people are coming than leaving, something must be working; we must be better than other places. Our rapid growth indicates a long-term optimism; we believe in a place enough to establish a home. Names of these new housing developments remind me of optimism of farmers and their fruit labels: Sunnyside Grove, Town and Country, The Highlands, Sun Villas.

My "good enough theory" manifests itself in our education system: we seem satisfied if we're near the fiftieth percentile in state test scores. Average is okay. I see this at graduation. Picture middle-school promotions where 30 percent of the students will drop out of high school, or high school ceremonies in light of the Valley's low rate of college attendance and retention towards a degree. Nonetheless, these festive graduations remain a rite of passage, a renewal of optimism. A celebration. We'd all make good farmers.

But I'm not completely satisfied

with life here and don't believe things should stay as they are. Optimism also implies things can be better. I'm still hungry for more, a quest to foster new hope for the Valley. Change is hard to come by here, though, and we often find comfort in the familiar—which also may contribute to our optimism.

The urban culture of the Bay Area or Los Angeles remains fast-moving, a future built on change. Such restlessness transplanted to our valley doesn't always work. We have a slower, constant rhythm that allows our communities to adjust. It's as if we need time for optimism to take hold. We make changes here because we are motivated more by positive indicators and feeling good. We're not so much prompted because things are so bad.

I heard a saying about the American South that may be applicable when substituting our valley. "When I'm about to die, I want to be in the Valley because change always happens here twenty years later." That's our twisted optimistic spirit, a wonderful humility.

Perhaps I too should reword my family farm fruit label to read "Grown with hope and trust: Don't worry, be happy."

Sincerely,
Mas

The Last Vineyard

Dear Dan,

   How does it feel to become obsolete? Farmers understand that emotion, especially when our old vineyards are no longer needed.

   You are now a retired farmer who ripped out a small vineyard of Grenache and Thompson grapes. It was harder and harder each year to find a crew to come pick those grapes; no one wanted to handle a small, five-acre block, even if you gave away the grapes. So a dozer came in, tore the vines from their roots, and now they're gone.

   You miss them—a little—and still long for some farm work. Your wife, Phyllis, says she looks out the kitchen window and hungers for the seasons: the bare vines in winter, the early shoots of spring, and the green blanket of summer. Now, it's just dirt.

   Dan, I also have old vines that I will tear out. Grape prices are not good. My vines aren't producing well. Every year requires more work to maintain them. The ninety-year-old trunks are gnarled and bent like old men. I sometimes accidentally hook them with my tractor and disk.

My old vineyard has an odd spacing pattern, eleven feet between rows instead of the standard of twelve. I imagine mules and old horse-drawn equipment didn't know the difference. Okay to squeeze in more vines per acre with a tight planting pattern. For me though, it was draining to constantly adjust equipment in order to fit the narrow rows. It grew harder and harder to weed between the twisted and contorted vines. I stopped taking care of them correctly, allowed more weeds to flourish and weak vines to grow weaker. I neglected them. They had grown obsolete.

Now, it's time to move on. A painful yet honest decision: keeping them was just not worth it. But I can't help feeling that I'm killing part of my spirit, too. It's not just a business decision. Those vines were something alive.

In my doomed vineyard lies a hidden memorial—the space where my father had his stroke while working the fields. His tractor suddenly jerked to one side and ripped out two vine trunks and roots. Later, I replanted them with the spirit that embodied his recovery. As he regained his strength, the new vines grew fast and thrived. Part of me remains superstitious: by killing those vines will I also somehow hurt my father?

Dan, how do others value a farmer's work? Apparently not much. Instead, everyone stopped to ask what you were going to do with the open land.

You shook your head and shrugged your shoulders, as if it was wrong not to develop the land.

"Better to grow houses," they said. (How bittersweet— the name of the housing tract across the street: Sanger Ranch.)

But for those who work the land and leave their mark on the earth, we have family memories invested in the landscape. In your case, you shared your fruits by making wine. Nothing fancy, but wine made for your fellow Italian countrymen and friends. A wine sold in one-gallon jugs that reminded others of their homeland. A simple dinner wine to drink daily with meals.

Jack, your son, remembered delivering the wine in a pick-up, bottles rattling as you drove from Hanford to Visalia, Sanger, Fresno, and Chowchilla. You made your rounds arriving with hardy wines, no cork required. You kept making the vintage for as long as you could, ignoring offers to sell to investors who sought to open a boutique winery.

Why? Because where else could your fellow Italian country folk get their wine?

I feel a loss when an old vineyard is terminated, as if part of history also disappears. Some of my old vines were planted in 1918, the year my grandmother journeyed from Japan to California. As the bulldozer marches in, I'll probably feel melancholy, and then try to move on by claiming, "Keeping the vines was too much work."

Yet I'll search for connections, acknowledging the passing of time while also looking to the future. I'll collect a few cuttings from my old vines and replant history, just as you still keep old jugs and wine labels.

Later, in my vacant field, I plan to try and create a natural habitat, a program to bring back native plants and wildlife and return the land to nature. I'll then extend a hearty thanks for letting our family borrow the land for a few decades while we grew memories.

Dan, you too have left behind stories, of some of the best wine an old Italian immigrant ever had: a taste of their homeland.

Our farms create physical reality checks for our families and neighbors, a public viewing of the obsolescence that we have accepted. But for you and me, our empty fields will be filled with the ghosts of farmworkers and farmers. Once, I saw you disking that field. You wore an old straw hat while driving an ancient, gray Ford with a tandem disk. You looked happy on that tractor. For a moment, you were once again working your fields.

Dan, you still managed to claim a little of the past by defiantly keeping two rows of grapes. Just enough to make wine for home use. And should they ever build houses on your property, I think they should name it Tuscany Estates in honor of your Italian roots. Perhaps both of us can join our family cultures and one day create our own special fusion brew—a sake grappa. I can picture us smacking our lips and toasting the past and future harvests.

Salute!
Kampai!
Mas

PART THREE

Learning Community

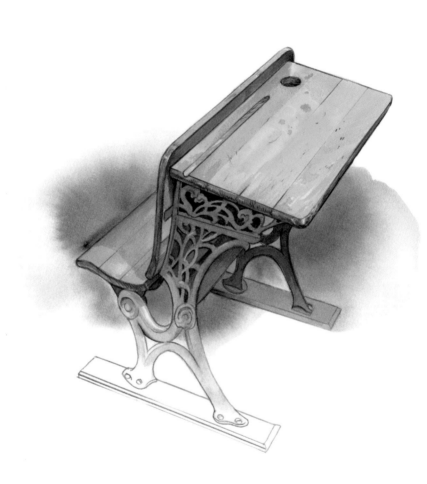

Community Graduations

Dear Mom,

Empty desks.

That's what you and thousands of Japanese American kids left behind at schools throughout the Central Valley in the fall of 1942, when the United States government defined families of Japanese ancestry as "the enemy" and exiled them from their homes and communities. Our family boarded trains for the Arizona desert and you spent four years imprisoned, living behind barbed wire.

You grew up in Fowler, a small town of a few thousand residents just south of Fresno. Our family were farmworkers, lived in town, traveled to the fields by day, returned home by night, and in between the kids squeezed in an education in the Fowler school system. A few in the family finished high school there, but you and Uncle George were exiled before you could graduate, torn from friends and a school they could call their own.

You finished high school at Canal Camp High at a place in Arizona that no longer exists; Gila River Relocation Center was quickly dismantled following the end of World War II. The military authorities felt an obligation to school the tens of thousands of children who looked like the enemy, so they created small school districts at each internment camp, schools for thousands of Nisei (second generation Japanese Americans, the majority of them American citizens). Years later you still have "Camp" high school reunions with your other Japanese American classmates, but you never returned to Fowler High because you never belonged. All you left behind was an empty desk.

From 1942 to 1945, absent from hundreds of June graduation ceremonies were Japanese American classmates. Now there's a movement to right this wrong. In 2004, Assembly Bill 781 retroactively offered you a diploma from the high school you would have been part of, a diploma that symbolizes more than simply completing the required classes. It also may carry meaning: a welcome home.

Mom, I'm not sure how I would have responded, separated from my friends, confused and terrified about being uprooted. You were only a high school freshman, frightened by the unfolding course of events, the youngest in a family of seven. Fowler was the only world you knew before being thrown into an unknown world, an instant city of ten thousand in the Arizona desert with new classmates who all looked like you.

Did you ever wonder about the school you left behind? Did fellow students miss you and the hundreds of other Nisei classmates? Your camp-school friends became special, and you all shared in a tragic yet historic episode of American history. Your camp graduation seemed as real as the one in Fowler.

But there was a difference: your diploma from Canal

Camp High symbolized an insane moment of prejudice, a harsh reminder of the racism of difference. You and tens of thousands suffered not from an individual, private act of discrimination, but a very public and wounding show of hatred when you, a little thirteen-year-old girl from a dusty farm town, became the enemy of the United States of America.

Public humiliation demands a public apology. That's what receiving your rightful diploma can mean: a public acknowledgment. Now, over sixty years later, your class of 1945 can march to the music of pomp and circumstance, in front of the Fowler community, knowing you finally belong.

❦

Once in a writing class I taught, I divided the class in half. On one side was a group of students who were part Asian. (It could have been any type of group: Catholic or Italian or left-handed.) I pretended to expel and relocate that one group, explaining they would be forced to leave the area without protest nor explanation. Before departing, however, they had to write a letter to a friend in the other half of the class, explaining what they would leave behind and to whom they'd give their pets or music collections or clothes. Those who received these gifts had to write a thank-you note, an awkward response to these unexpected acts from a friend they might never see again. The students were challenged with the assignment, some refusing to take it seriously, others unsure of their emotions. One wanted to kill his pets instead of leaving them behind; another refused to accept clothes from a friend who sounded like she was leaving to die. They struggled when we discussed graduation: they all had expected to be around and graduate as a class.

The students understood the ties that bind friendships, especially those formed in school. The value of a diploma extends beyond academics, the years in school can instill a powerful social dynamic that can connect and anchor students to a place. Meaning and memory are created.

Mom, when I think about relocation and your being denied a diploma from Fowler High, I can't help but think of a similar yet very different loss. Beyond your story, we still have empty desks in our schools today, lost students who too easily and quickly become invisible. While the circumstances are, of course, very different, thousands of empty desks are left behind every year from the huge numbers of students who drop out.

Some are very difficult cases, many are simply young kids lost. All bear some individual responsibility for lack of motivation, poor study skills, and bad choices. But are we as a community taking the value of a diploma for granted? I wonder if there's connection: a public humiliation we quietly struggle with, an embarrassment by such large drop-out rates of 30 to 40 percent in our schools.

Inevitably, this can become the basis for huge community problems of unemployment and poverty. And place matters with this problem. My sense is that dropouts tend to stay put and don't simply go away; after all, where can they go to with limited resources?

Public education remains a community responsibility. Just as you may feel finally "welcomed home" by receiving your Fowler High diploma, I wonder if we couldn't "welcome home" a huge class of youth back into our communities by drastically reducing dropout rates, and redoubling efforts and programs for those who already have dropped out and welcoming them back to school. The power of belonging, of claiming a place as your home, is part of the meaning of a diploma and the education of a people.

Your camp graduation—typically a time of hope, a rite of passage towards fulfilling a dream—was all so very different behind barbed wire. But a Fowler High graduation, though decades late, continues the journey home. And in a similar way, if we as a community can find ways to keep kids in school so they can share the moment with a tiny, seventy-seven-year-old Nisei woman, we can celebrate a healing ceremony; a moment to right some wrongs for the present and the future; a public remembering.

Your son,
Dave Mas

Coming Home

Dear Nikiko,

My daughter, you finished your first year at UC Berkeley and came back home for the summer, and I know you're anxious to get away again. I have sensed that you are impatient with life here in this valley and that changes seem slow—much too slow for an eighteen-year-old.

But I hope you can relax, can take it easy. You're still young (that's not your fault), and there's so much you still can learn. What I see as tradition, you see as small-town thinking; where I see stability, you see stubbornness. I believe we know who we are because we know where we are.

Love, Dad

🌱

Dear Dad,

Summer has been long; it has turned into an undesired delay, a quarantine. I am hungry for movement and change. I want to feel the energy of civil disobedience, public debates, personal challenges, and new viewpoints.

During my first year away, I missed the comfort of home. But I see comfort as dangerously bordering complacency. Home defines part of me, but how can I discover the hidden treasures of myself if I don't go away? From our farmhouse porch and my bedroom window, our nutrient rich soil, mature grapevines, and heirloom peach trees fill my view. I appreciate what our farm means to us, but sometimes I get lost in the greens and browns. I cannot see beyond our farm; it's as if the trees are hiding the world from me. Beyond our farm the coastal mountain ranges and Sierra Nevada surround our house. The geography of the Valley can confine, restrict, and insulate us from the outside—from new ideas, from a fast-changing world. I want to escape.

I crave change and growth. I want challenge and liberation. I'm tired of the taboos of the Valley. Is stability maintained by silenced voices? I want to be free to learn, free to question authority, free to experiment with ideas.

Love, Nikiko

🌱

Dear Nikiko,

Go find yourself at Berkeley, a world teeming with change and energy and radical ideals, where difference is celebrated and sought. That's not what you'd typically say about the Valley.

You're learning, about the world, about challenging all you've been taught, and questioning voices of authority. Eventually, the work you do will speak volumes about your character, and you will leave your mark through your actions. It takes time, you have much to learn, and then the world of work awaits you.

Love, Dad

Dear Dad,

I'm tired of being warned not to "let those people at Berkeley" influence me or being told "beware of Berzerkeley." College may be a cauldron of youth and difference, but I am not a kid, easily influenced and vulnerable. I chose to go to Berkeley, a new place, and I choose to go back.

After a year I feel as if I'm finding my voice, but here in the Valley I'm ordered to listen. It seems like dissent is unacceptable. Dad, you went to UC Berkeley, you went away. Do you feel bottled up here in this valley, as I do?

At Berkeley I feel safe. It is where I can question, cultivate my own identity, shower it with different nutrients. Freedom fertilizes, letting my conscience decide who I am.

Why do people question the validity of my choice to major in Women's Studies? They smirk: "What kind of job can you get with that?" They don't understand. I didn't go to college to get a job. I went away to find my life's work. I want to educate, activate, and change the world.

In the Valley, I feel rejected by old stereotypes, not taken seriously because I am young. I've seen the outside, I want to go away. Here I'm assumed to fit the old model. I need to go away to create. I seek a new way of life.

Love, Nikiko

Dear Nikiko,

I am growing old and tired. I have no regrets, I continue to love my work and maintain a passion for the land.

Stepping into the fields allows me to slip into my own world. The peaches and grapes grow fat despite my errors, they forgive my mistakes and we begin anew every spring. I work with and write about the story of seasons.

Yet I sometimes wonder how different my life would have been: a writer in the big city? Or should I have followed my calling and become an educator, helping to grow minds, nurture creativity, harvest understanding?

Instead I sweat too much in hundred-degree heat; my hands blister from battles with Johnson grass, fingers bleed from trying to repair old, broken equipment. I return to the farmhouse porch beaten and drained, knowing there's always more to do.

My work doesn't leave enough time for reflection, searching for my voice, exploring this valley for the truly good, exposing and purging the negative. From deep within a muse questions: Am I growing obsolete?

Love, Dad

♣

Dear Dad,

I want to unleash my passion. I want to embody freedom of expression, to shout, wear a smile, and even whisper. I want to shatter taboos. I will work in devotion to tolerance, acceptance, and equality. Regret will mean nothing.

With the knowledge I have gained, my dreams have changed. I see myself as a new freedom fighter, part of a new generation pushing limits and denying pessimism.

I anticipate my life's work with optimism, dreaming

that my impact can be as sweet and succulent as one of our peaches. Dad, I feel revolutionary.

Love, Nikiko

❧

Dear Nikiko,

After college when you begin a career, you will soon be challenged: how do you define value? Knowledge versus money, intentions versus resources, causes versus jobs—who you are measured by what you do.

The future of our valley is going to be based on change. Quality of life defined by what we value and defining what's important. Questioning should never be a sign of failure yet our valley is full of fools who beat down new ideas with little thought of their own. I now grow weary of them but often walk away, unwilling to fight, no longer willing to lose. I only have a few more harvests in me.

Daughter, I hope you can help us with this journey. Perhaps that's why I wanted you to leave. We all need to see the world beyond the mountains so we can know where to call home. Families need to have a home.

Like you, I ran away to explore, then returned to the farm. Your grandfather, with his simple wisdom, gave me the opportunity to come home by allowing me to leave.

Love, Dad

❧

Dear Dad,

You let me leave, giving me the opportunity to find home. I'll be back next summer.

Love, Nikiko

Delayed Gratification

Dear Marcy,

Have we made a mistake? Our two children are part of a new generation, often called "Gen Y" or "Echo Boomers," born between 1980 and 1995, children of us baby boomers. Our kids' world thrives on speed and new technologies, a high-octane life with instant satisfaction. Out here on the farm, have we punished our children by denying them immediate rewards, forcing them to accept delayed gratification?

I'm sounding old, but everything seems faster for this generation. Time is compressed: an MTV universe rich with visual graphics, rapid edits, and breathless pace; a video game arena of life with rapid stimulation and sudden reward or failure and little time for celebration or agony because a new game begins without a pause; new innovations no longer anticipated but expected; instant communication demanded.

I think of our children in an Alice in Wonderland setting where they have to run to stay in place. And to get anywhere, they simply have to run twice as fast. (Yet all this high energy can descend into sudden boredom due to years of training: Gen Y has practiced and perfected the art of the short attention span.)

Then I watch us morphing into "helicopter parents" who can't help but hover over our children. We structure their time—from school activities to weekend enrichment programs, from sports to competitive games. Toss in some music and arts in order to keep them balanced (others claim these activities look good on college applications), and we polish them into trophy children. We protect them from distractions and danger, overmanage and massage their moments, wanting them to have everything, fearful of blemishing their complete development.

We ask them to overachieve and want them to mirror us as multitaskers. Their lives are programmed for a mission of success. The best schools, the best lessons, the best teams and coaches—nothing but the best for this catered-to generation.

Whew. Our poor kids. Are they really that screwed up, like we parents can be? Time compression is loaded with a danger: it's all based on speed and increased pressure to succeed. Speed kills. When we falter in a fast world, we find the window for error is narrowed, the margin for mistakes almost nonexistent. Should we stumble, going that fast, we crash.

Marcy, how have we damaged our kids' psyche? We still believe in that old-fashioned theory: With hard work, good things happen. We make our kids work summers on the farm. While they spend much less time with chores than we did while growing up (me on a peach and grape farm, you on a goat dairy), I acknowledge that we worked much less than our parents on the farms of their childhood. Still, I catch myself claiming how easy our kids have it compared to "when I was growing up..."

But our children know about a type of work that's slow. Very slow. Painfully slow. Certainly nowhere close to a video game pace. Most things on the farm take their time. While I may be sprinting during the summer harvest, a lot of the time is spent monitoring and assessing, such as making sure I scrutinize the growth of weeds, which is about as slow as, well, watching paint dry.

So much for overstimulation. In this valley, we still cling to a slowness and perhaps that's why some families move here and claim it's a relaxing place to raise a family.

Out on the farm, our timelines are measured by seasons and years. I date events by when we planted an orchard: the Sun Crest peaches bore my siblings and myself through college; the Flavor Crest peaches grew tall when our son Korio started school, and the LeGrand nectarines were reintroduced to our fields just as daughter Nikiko left for college. I hope the children remember this language of the past as they embark on their own futures.

We also allowed the kids to fail at times. Remember the grand garden we planted, proud farmer parents beaming at Nikiko's lush squash plants? Then a virus attacked and some of the plants withered. I wanted to spray something for a quick fix, not quite the message an organic farmer wanted to send. So we let them die. But the wise child taught the father a lesson: "Don't worry dad, we have other plants."

I enjoyed watching the children when they played

alone, occupying themselves without orchestrated events, a necessity due to the curse for farm kids—neighbor kids may be miles away, you have to schedule a visit with friends. Urban families seem to fill playtime with organized sports and structured activities. But can't play just be play?

And Korio, now in the seventh grade, has learned a lesson that took me decades to comprehend about myself: he's not good at everything, nor does he need to be. He's learned to go slow on a tractor because he's more comfortable taking his time; he doesn't need to be wild and aggressive nor always going fast. Contrast that to an education system that is increasingly based on speed, and he's securing a place for himself—confident enough to be himself no matter what his scores insinuate.

Our kids may be technologically challenged. We do have computers and cell phones but our phone lines are slow, and years ago I used to tell the kids we couldn't get cable because we were out on a farm. Then Korio noticed all the satellite dishes and my excuse crumbled. But our lives are not centered around television. During dinner we still look at each other. (Although I will admit, when we go on vacation, I thoroughly enjoy a hundred channels to choose from and will stay up late in the hotel room just so I can surf channels. At least I do this with my children. We bond.)

I do try to put changes with technology in historical context. The speed of computing, access to information, even the language of e-mail (omg—oh my god, or pos—parents over shoulder) shouldn't warp our kids too much.

I imagine our parents said the same thing about all the television we began watching in the fifties and sixties, and our grandparents worried about the time our parents wasted listening to the radio or reading pulp fiction. Somehow, with all this speed and new innovations, the kids are probably going to turn out fine.

Marcy, I do worry about a few things. All this stimulation can be overwhelming. Not enough time for thinking, little opportunity to pause before reacting, no chance to ponder before answering. Consider that the state and national school testing programs are based on speed and quick responses—it's no wonder our children have little experience in reflection.

I've heard kids who don't seem to trust their own voices. They've spent so much time memorizing and processing information, they have lost their own confidence. When they don't believe in their own story, they deny themselves an identity and feel worthless. That's a tragedy.

Kids then drop out. They start "doing time" in activities where they become invisible. I've driven in a van taking kids to summer camp and instead of chatter and excitement, they're all listening to Walkmans, lost in their own worlds. Hanging out, doing video games, mindlessly surfing TV, nondirected time-consuming activities: is this unhealthy, non-productive time? Or perhaps I just don't get it: do today's kids need time to escape and "check out" for a while? Then are we parents too driven? Can you hear the hum of helicopter rotors as we hover?

I do fear a loss of creative spirit. Maybe our kids are

getting too good at mastering the program; learning to do what's required, responding to the demands of the system. They accept the rules and aim to please. Sometimes, I am happy when our children complain about life on the farm. It shows they're engaged enough to care, willing to verbalize their feelings, no different than we were.

I chuckle at what an old farmer once shared with me: "My folks were old-fashioned and believed in the work ethic so much, I swear, they planted weeds to make sure I had enough work to do."

We haven't resorted to planting weeds, but sometimes, I believe we are starting to look like our own parents. They allowed us to be ourselves: country kids. And maybe that's not bad.

Love,
Mas

Rejection Letters

Dear Nikiko,

Two years ago, my daughter, during your senior year of high school, you were fortunate enough to receive a big, fat envelope in March—your college acceptance.

Families throughout the country awaited these letters, a rite of passage, a turning point in a student's life. With acceptance came the potential of a college education, a future filled with hope and the statistical reality: college graduates earn about $15,000 more each year, or a million dollars in a lifetime, than those holding only a high school diploma. Imagine receiving a million-dollar letter! And for many here in the Central Valley, big fat envelopes meant that for the first time, someone in a family won the lottery: the chance to go to college.

Or not.

For many seniors, there were no fat envelopes. Higher education's share of the state budget has been shrinking, and less money translates into fewer spots on campus and higher fees for those admitted. The door closes to thousands of eligible California students who were denied access after years of promises: "With hard work, there will be a spot for you at our college table."

Granted, the public has been contributing to increased funding of education with a new emphasis on kindergarten through twelfth grade. But this overlooks higher education. We seem to have been operating under the assumption that college opportunity would always be there. Tell that to your classmates who should have joined you on campus or to your Valley friends discouraged by the increase in tuition and fees.

All the while, our state's population increases by 2 percent each year, generating more, not less, demand for college.

Niki, we're sending a message of rejection to your generation: We don't want you. Perhaps colleges needed to send a different sort of letter in March. Instead of big, fat envelopes, they could send a skinny letter in April: "Congratulations. A few years ago, you could have joined us but today we have to reject you. Not because you didn't meet our high standards, not because you didn't do what we asked. Rather, it's because we don't have the money."

Do students feel betrayed? At a time of increasing demand by eligible students and growth in college applications, we should be increasing availability. Instead we play a game of Catch-22, seemingly implying that we now want brighter students for spots at our public institutions of higher education, and that others are not welcomed. For hundreds of students who could have been the first generation in their family to attend college, is their California dream tarnished? Do they blame themselves, depressed because they didn't get high enough grades or test scores?

Niki, at your ten-year high school reunion, will your peers still be struggling to complete college degrees because classes weren't offered? Will they have left for states that welcomed them? (In Oregon, colleges already have seen an increase in applications from California.) Some may feel trapped, unable to get ahead because the great vehicle of mobility—education—doesn't have a space for them or was too expensive. This trickles down to the community college level. Overwhelmed by demand for limited slots, Fresno City College has resorted to a random selection process to enter its nursing program—education by lottery.

We shouldn't tolerate this and I hope there's a public outcry. I hope we don't target the state's colleges and universities, but rather blame ourselves. We, the public, are sending these rejection letters to high school seniors and community college transfers: We don't recognize how bright you are and we don't support you. We distance ourselves, some taking comfort in the fortune our families may have already had in benefiting from California's higher education master plan. We don't feel the disappointment, and we rationalize that this is a problem for children of other families, other ethnic groups, other classes, other geographies. We don't see these students as our kids.

We need to reclaim ownership and personalize the impact of reducing educational opportunity. Imagine, as we baby boomers grow older: where's the nurse we need, lost in a lottery? Who will teach our grandkids, with some of the best young educators chased off to other states? Here in the Central Valley, will we be doomed to become a Mecca of crummy jobs because we have an uneducated workforce?

We helped write rejection letters to your classmates by allowing the issue to drift far off our radar screens. We have too easily accepted the devaluing of our state's higher education system—our own version of March madness. In April, many are reeling from rejection, believing the public doesn't care about the future, is willing to dumb down the state's youth and restrain a new generation's potential. We deny education to those who are qualified as if we don't trust them. Unknowingly, we may be planting seeds to crush our future.

I'm sorry and hope we can fix this by demanding more funds for public higher education and, soon, sending more big, fat envelopes of opportunity.

Your father

Send Money

Dear Fred,

In college, I used to begin conversations with my folks simply, directly: Send money. I relied on their benevolence to help me out. Now that I'm older, the thing I ask, though directed differently, remains simple: community groups need people to send money. It's called philanthropy and it can make us feel good.

You're a successful businessman and no one should tell you or anyone what to do with their money. But consider this a suggestion, a consideration, a hope for our valley's future: Have you thought of giving away a lot more of your money?

You've already supported numerous causes and local community groups. People know you're generous and a model citizen. Yet after you're gone, can your good will stay in the Valley?

Compared with the nation (and especially the East Coast), our valley communities are young, only a few generations old. And most people here have earned, not inherited their wealth. While individuals have supported fund-raising efforts for schools, nonprofit organizations, and churches, we lack consistent and ongoing large-scale support. We don't have many family or corporate foundations, and we haven't attracted many large, outside foundations to give, despite our needs.

With struggling governmental budgets, public sector help is doubtful. We must take care of things ourselves, we must address our big needs with big giving. We need a culture of philanthropy—giving because we want to, sending money to fix things and to feel good.

I'm talking about giving away our hard-earned money. I used to think only the wealthy practiced philanthropy; something for the super-rich with millions of dollars lying around. But I'm rethinking my own giving: smaller gifts, a few thousands of dollars, or a family gift of tens of thousands of dollars can work miracles here. In our valley we're used to not getting much, so we've learned to do wonders with little.

Philanthropy is about giving away excess wealth—something most will claim we don't have. Whether we work for low wages or are rich, we think of excess wealth as "what's left over," and who really has any of that?

Wealth isn't always defined by money. I've witnessed many who have very little income yet are very, very generous with another kind of wealth: their time. They contribute by volunteering, organizing programs, showing up to do the grunt work. We're all better off due to their philanthropy.

Still, many in the Valley middle and upper classes don't think of themselves as monetary philanthropists. Few have any idea of what our money means to us. Until that's addressed, it's impossible to have excess wealth.

Philanthropic giving is about the important things we leave behind—not material things, but something with value. Taking care of family and heirs, of course, remains essential. But sometimes I wonder how much my children will really need or want? The value I leave isn't in dollars and cents, rather is measured in memories and stories. Giving is the difference between being successful and elevating ourselves to significance.

Fred, here's my two-generation theory about family: how many remember our father's and mother's first names? Probably most of us. How about our grandfather and grandmother? Still, most likely, many of us. But how about our great-grandparents? Most only have two-generation knowledge of our heritage and, within a short time, you and I will probably be forgotten. It's pretty easy to die with insignificance, and that sounds tragic to me.

We can leave behind value—the tremendous feeling of giving wealth for the benefit of others. The human spirit of giving creates stories that last for generations. The business of legacy—I like the sound of that.

A family foundation expert once explained that there's really only four places money can go: one, we spend it on ourselves; two, the government inherits it; three, we give it to family and friends; or four, we can send money. Many of us are fairly comfortable; we spend what we need to on ourselves. I doubt if many of us want to give our wealth to the government voluntarily. With family and friends, the real question isn't the distribution of money, but the distribution of values. Most of us yearn to be good people, and giving remains one of the greatest acts of kindness.

We in the Valley are at that next stage of development: fostering a culture of givers. We can measure the health of our communities by what is given back, we can show the world how we take care of things ourselves. Philanthropy is one indicator of people investing in themselves and in places they value. We become defined by what we give.

To build a culture of givers requires leadership, those with long-term vision and who set aside funds not only for one-time giving, but forever. I think contributing to community foundations—organizations that pool donors' gifts and fund a variety of projects and programs—or creating family foundations can begin to build a consciousness of caring over the long haul. Wealth then stays home in the Valley in a highly visible way: we build the infrastructure for consistent and continued giving; to make a bigger pie for everyone's benefit.

Historically, only a few large foundations have given to our valley. The Irvine Foundation, which I'm involved with, may be an exception. In 2003, it dedicated $10 million to the Valley and, from it, I've learned a few lessons.

First, giving to organizations helps legitimate the value of those programs. It's as if we in the Valley lack confidence in our stories and the good work of many community groups. Gifts, sometimes from outside the community, validate our worth.

Second, giving is part of a slow-money approach to the local economy—investments in people and places with the expectation that results will take years to become visible. Returns are then measured in terms of quality of life, not profit margins. As our valley evolves economically, our social capital, the personal relationships that glue us together, can also grow. We learn to do things for each other.

Third, giving can inspire. I hope the Irvine Foundation's work breeds new funders from the Valley. As community foundations are formed and strengthened, as individual family foundations are created, I hope a new generation of givers is born. Giving money can become contagious, dollars cycled back into our communities may work as a multiplier, generating added giving from others. It's not about what our valley needs, but what we need to do; it's not about asking, but wanting to give.

Philanthropy requires us to think in plurals. We're the "other California" and we can differentiate ourselves by becoming a valley of kind acts, doing the right thing by recognizing things worth saving, surprising and inspiring ourselves by teaching and building a culture of philanthropy right here. Yes, right here in this valley. When we have unconditional love for a place and its people, we send money.

Thanks,
Mas

Leaving Home

Dear Nikiko,

I'll miss you, my daughter, as you leave home to study in Mexico for a year. I know that was the reason why for the last month I became a "helicopter parent," hovering over you, checking and rechecking your travel arrangements and flight times, and contacting people about your departure even when you didn't ask (or perhaps didn't want me to).

I'll miss you just as parents do when their children leave for college, for work, for new places far away from home, far away from family. I now sense an emptiness, a void, and can't help but think of you when I see the empty chair at the dinner table or walk by a vacant bedroom or see something that reminds me of you—a toothbrush, a pair of shoes, a family photograph. I miss the times when your voice would have filled the room or times in the shed where we packed peaches and you would have been helping. The moments we were family.

Without you, our house will not seem the same even with Korio, your younger brother, still at home. You may very well never be the same.

Technically, you left two years ago for the University

of California, Berkeley. Mexico—with your studies in Monterrey, Mexico City, and eventually Oaxaca—is one more step in your journey. I can't imagine the emotions a parent feels when a child makes a single leap all at once: moving out of home, getting married, studying in another state, settling in another land. (The death of a child must be a thousand times harder.)

But moving to another country makes you seem even farther away. I know from my own experience as an exchange student to Japan, each step holds the potential to become a major turning point in life.

As you leave home, I sense we may be losing you. Will you return to the farm or continue the phenomenon of modern agriculture and the exodus of youth from working the land? Once you leave, is it true you can never go home again? I remember when I ran away from this narrow valley, wanting to venture beyond the mountains and escape to see, feel, and taste other places. My dad had a wisdom I hope I can mimic: by letting me go away, he allowed me to come home.

I recognize that change is necessary and youth often thrives on the new. But I'm discovering that as I get older, I enjoy a slower pace and it's nice for things to change gradually. I know this is unrealistic, yet it's real: slow can be just fine and rapid change, while beneficial, can also be draining. Take your time, think a lot.

Nikiko, you have started your own magical journey as an entire new world opens before you. I see my road ahead differently: life is not so bright, not all change is good. I'll watch my parents continue to age and then pass away.

Health concerns will gradually fill more of my thoughts and affect my lifestyle. My work and career don't have paths full of opportunity like yours. Some of my peers are finishing their career journeys, others hang on until retirement. Many of us ask: did we achieve our potential and make the most of our lives? It's a haunting question.

I see you facing a series of life-altering decisions, choices you've begun to make. You may not see their impact until later when you look in life's rearview mirror and recognize the things that mattered.

Living abroad, will you return with different consciousness? A global sense of the world while you learn of another culture? I'm pleased you're in Mexico and can experience lessons that will prepare you for what some call the "Latinization" of California and the nation. Knowing Spanish will only positively affect career, community work, and friendships. (A regret I have endured, a world closed to me because my Spanish is so poor.)

Traveling and living in a foreign country will imprint images you'll never forget: the poverty and hope, the class dynamics and struggle, the strength of community and family woven into a different social fabric. And you'll be treated like an outsider, the gringa, the one who is different. Will you see the ugly American, those who impose their will on others? Will you begin to question things our nation does and you're not proud of? Or will you see our country as a land of promise and hope, the "El Norte" power casting a broad shadow on the people south of our border?

I now know what I must leave behind. To live with a false hope that nothing changes in life will result in little gained in life. Besides, we can travel to visit you and who knows, you may learn to appreciate home more. You may even miss us.

I'm happy for you and I'm proud that you are seizing the day. And I hope, in the future, you will manage to come home for part of a summer and work on the farm even for a few days. We can then renew the feeling of a family farm.

I remember stories when your mom was a young adult and would travel home to milk goats on their farm, spend Christmas vacation cleaning out a pen, shoveling manure, being part of a family. Or in church, her parents would proudly beam when all the children were sitting in the same pew, all gathered together.

Are these fleeting memories of a life we can never relive? Or do we celebrate those moments when all seems whole again?

So how do we say good-bye?

You are no longer the child who leaves home, and now perhaps you can become my friend. And yet you will forever remain my daughter.

Love you,
Your dad

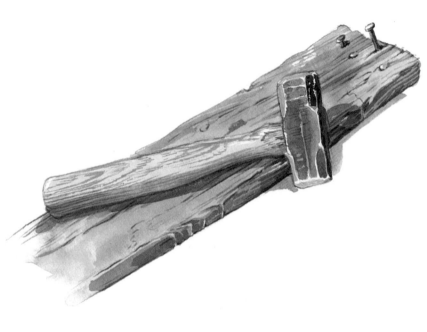

Good Enough Theory

Dear Nikiko,

Don't come home, my daughter. You've left for college at UC Berkeley and I'm not sure you should return. A "good enough" mentality thrives in our valley. Life is comfortable here, a good place to raise a family and be happy. Okay is fine for most; things remain good enough because people rarely ask for more. If you come home, I fear you'll long for things we don't have.

Good enough means things aren't that bad, which then implies that things must be good. As if being at the 50th percentile means you're better than others, at least half the others. And what's wrong with that?

A few years ago, an "outsider" school superintendent arrived at a local school and questioned the district's "average" test scores. Teachers and parents responded: scores were at the 50th percentile, recently raised by five points! The superintendent was eventually run out of town.

We create communities of the comfortable, and the tension found in big cities seems lacking here. I'm not sure if we're blind to realities or we do a great job of designing communities to avoid seeing inequalities. Freeways function as convenient, modern-day blinders as thousands drive past poverty and bad neighborhoods, and are insulated from "those people" with problems. (Instead, I like riding the train, which takes me past the backyards of Valley towns, where the poor can't be hidden. It's like touring another world, an uncomfortable world.)

In the Valley, a suburban mentality seems to dominate. People want neighborhoods that look more or less the same because sameness equates to contentment and a security in numbers. We're all generally happy (or all equally unhappy) with an emphasis on "all." Neighbors worry about sports, the price of gas, the next movie release, and the politics of saying "Happy Holidays" instead of "Merry Christmas." We seem to lack a focus on fundamental local issues and can't tackle the big ones, accepting a 30 percent high school drop-out rate and tolerating rampant poverty that labels us as the new Appalachia.

Lurking beneath the benign "good enough" thinking may be something more sinister: an inability to accept difference. It reminds me of the Japanese saying: A nail sticking out should be pounded back in place. Nikiko, whenever you come home, even just to visit, you'll be challenged to label yourself here. Are you part of the radical left (a student from UC "Berzerkeley")? Or are you guilty by association and entrenched on the right because you're from a farm family out in rural America, part of those "red" areas that vote conservative.

Perhaps "intolerance of change" is too strongly worded. Rather, we often simply ignore difference. People and places remain invisible in our valley, lost in the winter fog, withering in the summer heat. Ghosts dot the landscape: the poor, those who struggle in our educational systems, non-English speakers, undocumented workers, laborers at minimum paying jobs.

We tolerate them with an indifference that equates to complacency. It all fits a good-enough rhythm. Excellence is rarely sought. We ask why and not why not. Our battle cry: We demand a little more good! Greatness? That's reserved for other places.

❧

Nikiko, I must admit that life is much simpler when you believe in "good enough." If you work hard, why shouldn't there be a reward of comfort instead of struggle? At certain points, people grow weary of trying to raise the bar and are content with being okay. A "don't worry, be happy" mentality is much less stressful. I sleep better at night, I'm not as angry. I may live longer with acceptance instead of dying young fighting something unwinnable.

Do I appear happier? Perhaps. I'm not as lonely, I fit into crowds better here, and I walk around with a strange look of satisfaction. Maybe that's just fine. Out on our farm, hidden from problems, have I discovered Iowa in the Valley? And what's wrong with being comfortable? All I ask is to do my best and if my best is just fair, I can live with that. I've earned the right to be just okay and satisfied. Don't equate not choosing to be involved with not caring.

Should we in the Valley continue to be defined by what we are not? Let's ignore the agrarian past. After all, isn't this place more than peaches and raisins, and who'd want to become a farmer? The economic depression of Appalachia is rooted in mining, so to throw off the shackles of poverty shouldn't we dispose of farms and agriculture?

Yet we continue to build places that look alike, because we're not sure what a "Fresno look" is. Clearly, for Fresno, there is no "there" there. But here's the question: Do we even want a "there"? (A history lesson here: remember all the jokes about the new city hall design?) Consider the recent portrait of the young cultural entrepreneurs of Fresno in battle with us old folks who are entrenched in our ways. We just don't "get it" with arts and entertainment do we? Bohemia in Fresno with the help of City Hall sounds like a contradiction to me.

Or am I in denial? Shouldn't the question be: How do we make good enough better? We can begin by taking care of what we have—a slower culture, built on a regional perspective, with a strong working-class mentality, diverse and mixed ethnically. Then add a will to be great and we begin to grow up. But first we need to go beyond good enough.

So perhaps in my next letter to you, my daughter, I should explore the reasons why you should come home.

Love,
Your father

Telling the Truth in the Valley

Dear Nikiko,

You need to come home, my daughter. Truths need to be told that can promote action and change. But sometimes it's hard to be honest in this valley; telling the truth can create distrust.

If you come back after graduating college, you'll enter into a culture of affirmation. Many of us listen to those who agree with us; to be analytical equates to criticism. The right listens to their political pundits found on talk radio. Somehow what Sean Hannity or Rush Limbaugh says is automatically appropriate for the Valley.

Meanwhile, the left seeks their sources as a rebuttal to the establishment. They listen to Bill Moyers or Pacifica Radio shedding the light on truth.

Rarely do they listen to each other. You'll never see a "dittohead" listening to NPR or coffee shop farmers gathered around the broadcast of KPFA's election coverage.

Within this climate, it's hard to be critical in a constructive way. Instead, mistakes are quickly classified as failures and errors are rarely admitted. I've seen public policy decisions become personal. Recall elections become commonplace, confrontational politics rule.

Then the best leaders seem to run from public service and I don't blame them. A writer once observed that in small towns, the discussions become vicious because there's so little at stake.

I, too, have caught myself worrying about personalities instead of asking hard questions. That's why I hope you come home. We need new, young voices with a willingness to talk instead of confront.

Will you be bold enough to speak of excellence for all? In the past, when you visited from college, you were quick to point out the invisible: the poor and the underclass of our valley.

At times, I had slipped into a trance and accepted their plight without question. I concluded the Valley, a Mecca for crummy jobs, will always have the poor. I pointed out the efforts to create workers for a new economy and then realized: Why not strive for more at all levels? We can campaign for both: jobs that call for increasing knowledge and, at the same time, jobs, any jobs, even those at minimum wage. Those offering entry-level jobs, albeit low-paying, do not necessarily exploit and oppress. Who else will champion the needs of the underclass?

I've always thought of our Valley as a scattering of villages, many historically founded by ethnic groups. As time passed, the ethnic enclaves have changed and cities have grown, but a village mentality still exists rather than a regional perspective.

Thinking regionally would require someone in Fresno to actually worry about Del Rey or Sanger and vice versa. But why? Does life in Reedley and Kerman really affect north Fresno? What does Madera have to do with Visalia?

Someone once told me, "You live so far out in the country and it takes so long to get to your place, it all begins to look the same." I'm guilty of saying that about their housing tracts in Clovis.

Nikiko, I hope you'll return to offer advice and not opinion. Opinion sounds too easy, often not requiring much thought. We have lots of opinions in this valley; what I want is advice. I hope that implies careful reflection and a decision to take responsibility. I'll find it refreshing to have someone say something and not only mean it, but accompany it with action. Advice implies commitment.

The Valley misses a critical center where people trust both sides. We lack a community conversation and instead respond with a crisis management mentality. Often, only with a major threat do we take action. And when that threat is averted, we feel good about ourselves and move to the next crisis, forgetting the source of the problem and how to address structural change or reform.

I've found this true with local school politics—especially when union contracts are up for renewal. Talk of crises during negotiations seem to suddenly dissipate with agreement. Contracts are signed and schools return to normalcy with a happy face.

I hope you will be brave enough to speak of excellence and shake up the status quo. Of course, the gamble is that perhaps I'm part of the problematic status quo and the things you want to fight for might not be the same as mine. But I ask you to come back and I will try to accept who you are. And if one more Valley person says, "I hope Berkeley didn't ruin you," I'll shake my head and won't blame you for leaving.

The draw for you to come home isn't a new downtown entertainment center or nightlife in the city. I ask you to come back because we need you. You've grown up and you're not just a kid anymore. That's good.

Your dad

Who Owns a River?

Dear John,

   While we were floating the lower Kings River in kayaks, I got to thinking: who owns this river?

   You love this river and live along a beautiful section where the current snakes gracefully past farmlands. You have spent many hours on the water and now devote energy to forming an organization, the Kings River Conservancy, to protect and open the river to the public.

   But who owns this water and its rapids and gentle currents, the rocks and boulders, the trees and grassy banks, the fish and flora? Who claims the sounds of rushing water, bird calls, and the silence that lingers around a slow bend in the river? We all do.

   Certainly landowners along the river can claim that their property line extends to the middle of the waterway. However, many rivers, including the Kings, do allow for recreational use. I am not trespassing as I ride the river's current past the shade of cottonwoods or awkwardly bounce over and through part of a fallen tree. Landowners certainly have property rights; I'd be wrong if I pulled up on the bank and onto land, but that's not the purpose of floating the Kings, is it? Staying in the water seems fine to me.

Yet, few speak about the responsibility river landowners have: the majority of property is zoned agricultural and I believe they should leave the bank along the river in its natural state. As a farmer, I know you can't farm those few yards along a river without major headaches: equipment gets stuck; tractors work at dangerously steep angles; farm fertilizers and chemicals threaten to contaminate a natural waterway; or the high water table drowns most farm crops. I don't think that's asking too much, to keep a river natural.

John, this may sound crazy, but floating the Kings made me think of the Information Age we live in. A river, with its natural splendor and powerful current of history etched into the banks, can be part of the new knowledge economy. We can own a river not necessarily by purchasing land but rather by knowing the story of that waterway and claiming that story as ours.

In this age of technology and information systems, knowledge becomes a product and the use of that knowledge can produce value. The more people know about a natural resource, like a river, the more connections they have and the more they acquire a type of ownership.

A broad view of the Kings River acknowledges the upper Kings, with its whitewater rafters and fly fishermen; Pine Flat Dam, with its assorted recreational users; and those that fish, float, or boat the lower Kings. We welcome the large network of participants. We share this river with thousands of others every year.

Add to that, those who directly benefit and take something away from the Kings. I remember fishing with buddies catching and eating trout (we also caught sucker and squawfish but no one bragged about that). We acted as if the river was home to "our" fish (including the "ones that got away").

In addition, thousands of farmers across the Valley take precious water from the Kings, a life-giving resource that makes this valley green and generates billions of dollars' worth of produce. How long could we farm just by pumping groundwater? The added economic expense and the tapping of a limited supply would have created a very different system: communities would have died long ago when the water dried up. We owe the river much, just as much as we take from her.

Finally, the story of the Kings is incomplete unless we include the story of those who have used it. We have floated the Kings on tire tubes, canoes, kayaks, and rafts. We have boated the Kings on powerboats, fishing boats, and party boats. We have played on beaches (yes beaches, albeit small, but still a place where the water and land gently meet) in numerous spots, some known only to a few. We own the Kings because we have memory.

We have memories of family and friends on the river, of parties and long lazy afternoons and evenings, of cold crisp mornings when the fish were biting, or scorching summer days when the snowmelt water from the mountains rushed down riverbeds and cooled our overheated bodies. We remember floating the Kings as high school kids, a fond time of innocence that seemed to match the slower pace of the river. We can recall the smell and taste of the river, the sounds of water and critters, the lightheaded daze of too much sun and beverages while on the water. Many own a history with this river.

We are connected to the Kings by stories, tales from our past and present. We own the river through the shares of information we have gathered as if we're all limited partners working together as a larger entity. By knowing and sharing our personal stories, we can claim a river to be ours.

A question looms for the future: how do we develop "our" river? How do we make it more accessible, encouraging more usage for all, and creating another generation of memories? Is it possible to balance the needs of property owners with us "shareholders" who use and enjoy the river, all the while keeping it as natural as possible, to ensure that the river remains a river?

You and others are working towards that goal, contributing to the growing story of a river and her people, helping generations to see what a river can be. Thanks for helping "my" river.

Mas Masumoto

PART FOUR

Going Slow

Caregivers

Dear Mom,

I watch your hands grow old. After Dad had his major stroke eight years ago, and now with his most recent setback, you care for this eighty-two-year-old man, making sure he doesn't fall, helping him clean up in the bathroom, monitoring his diet and medications—every morning, every evening, every day.

Hands that wash, lift, and clean. Hands that hold.

While Dad could be worse and his physical needs much more demanding, you probably haven't slept through the night in months, jumping up in a moment of panic when he stirs, fearing the worst, anticipating his needs. Some of the little things become daily challenges and they drain you both of life. I watch helplessly, accepting the reality that things won't get better.

You're part of an invisible corps of "caregivers," a reliable army of workers who help others with their day-to-day needs, often in their homes. Some are professionals, such as occupational or physical therapists who work with those who have been broken, repairing damage. Most are relatives: a spouse caring for a loved one; a sister or brother assisting a sibling; children reversing roles to nurture and care for aging parents. The vast majority are women—wives and daughters who give up their lives to fill a need. Few are paid, their deeds too often unnoticed; they labor quietly, asking little in return. They work because it's family.

Hands that cook, mend, carry, and support. Hand labor.

Nothing in your life prepared you for this. Suddenly you've been placed in a role of decision making, trying to determine what's the best for Dad. We try to work as family, all us kids supporting you. But like many caregivers, you feel odd "delegating love," so you carry much of the burden.

I feel caught in the middle too, part of the "sandwich generation"—raising my own children and now caring for aging parents. I know your sense of responsibility, torn between needs of others and yourself, balancing the needs of the many. There is a tragic difference: I can see a future with our children and with Dad the future looks dark.

I once resented those who offered unsolicited advice, but didn't know the daily realities of caregivers. I used to get angry at peers who escaped this valley, leaving their parents and the task of caring for the old to someone else. I felt left behind to bury the dead. After watching you, I understand choices we make and how I can't change others. I'm learning to purge myself of the negatives.

As in most families, not everyone gives the same. A son or daughter, a brother or sister may live far away and seem disconnected, yet they may harbor a guilt I'm not to judge. You once astutely said, "Doesn't bother me too much, I have enough to worry about."

Wise hands. Understanding hands. Nurturing hands.

You have simple goals: waking up to take care of the little things; daily survival in a world that sometimes spins out of control; going to sleep at night hoping you did your best. On good days, you can slip back into your old life, shopping and doing your town errands, making a special after-school snack for your grandson, or even take a day off to go gambling and escape for a few hours. But caregivers quickly return, knowing the difference between their public face and hidden private reality.

Farming has helped me understand how to take care of things and live with nature. I learned of long-term commitment and unexpected results. Ironically—in a new age of information, high technology and the rapid speed of change—a family-farm metaphor seems to work the best when caring for Dad: where things are slow, expectations humbling, and work fosters humility. You and Dad planned to stay put and grow old together, finding peace in a place called home.

Hands that work, steer, guide, prune, shape, and renew. Hands that know the earth and respect the land.

The fastest growing segment of the population are those over eighty-five. Our valley has an even higher number, as youth have left the farms while many newcomers settle here to retire. Perhaps our agrarian roots give us an advantage: we know well the gradual pace of small-town life, and even life in larger cities; we understand the meaning of those who plant roots. As the old shift from a life of independence, we may be well positioned to adopt a culture of dependence in which we take pride in taking care of each other.

Slow hands. Steady hands.

Yet talking openly about aging makes many feel uncomfortable. Families feel these are private matters. But growing old shouldn't be hidden, nor should caring be a secret. It's time we stop whispering about caregivers: honor them, their work, and the opportunities in our valley—a good place to grow old.

Hands that bleed, crack, bruise, break, and heal. Calloused hands.

Growing old can be lonely, our challenge is how we respond. Mom, you demonstrate your love and speak loudly by your caring. You have permission to take some breaks, to get angry and depressed, to ask for face time with family members and not just phone calls. It's okay to ask for help and it's okay to be yourself. Dad knows your hands, trusts your hands, loves your hands.

Hands that care. Hands that give.

Your son,
Dave Mas

Walking on Uneven Ground

Dear Dad,

I remember that after your stroke years ago, you had to learn how to walk on uneven ground.

Relearning something is among life's hardest challenges. It's like flunking a class: you have to repeat it and the rest of the world moves on while you are held back. The terms "slow" and "lazy" start to creep into your mind.

Relearning, however, has nothing to do with laziness or intellect. In fact, you had to work harder than you ever had in your life, desperately trying to reclaim something that was stolen from you. It would have been easier if the only problem from the stroke was walking. You also lost your speech, much of the right side of your body no longer worked, and things just took longer to comprehend. But as an old farmer, being able to walk became your goal. It represented a type of independence and freedom, and the opportunity to go home, back to the land.

The stroke insulted your body and mind, robbed you of skills and blurred your abilities. The first six months would determine what would "come back" or what would be forever lost. How you responded to the "insult" would determine your recovery. Waiting for things to heal didn't fit the scenario. Strokes demand patience accompanied with a fierce drive to work on relearning simple things: how to hold a spoon or pencil, how to roll upright and get out of bed, how to feel your right foot. One must acknowledge the loss and respond.

Quickly, old beliefs and false images dissolved (therapy is something only for the weak and disabled). Family became your support team and coaches, specialists taught you the essential yet seemingly little things that overwhelmed: "Pick up your foot; heel to toe, heel to toe strides; lift your knee to pull up a foot, don't forget to bend your knee." Your foot still dragged, you forgot it wasn't working. Pay attention and focus—a new universe of limitations.

You tackled these steps with a commitment to get better, grateful for little things and balancing expectations with reality. Remember: keep your foot in line, don't get lazy and swing your leg out wildly; learn to walk straight.

You had to depend on others, something many men struggle with. Lean on someone, literally and emotionally. Listen and correct, trust them and you learn to trust yourself. It's an odd way of learning. You were used to self-sufficiency and that's how our education is traditionally done. Collaboration in school is called cheating.

Some people around you felt sorry: "I hear your dad can't walk and can't talk." I answer, "He's getting better—or at least isn't getting worse." Then snap, "He's not dead, you know."

Separate the world: those who understand with empathy versus misplaced sympathy. It's no different than most other things—a world divided into "haves" and "have-nots." Dad, our family probably always belonged with the have-nots and that suits me fine; we're always hungry to learn and get better.

So we all learned about a slow world, learning to walk first. Bend your knee, heel to toe, pay attention—a stride out of synch with a fast-paced, high-tech, digital world. Farming always has been slower, our work seemingly out of rhythm, too. Has walking the fields become an obsolete practice?

I might sound old, but have you ever considered "slow" as being right and better, and "fast" as insulting? Rush to go, go, go in order to reach places quicker, only to be blinded by speed? Too fast to think, racing through thoughts, never slowing to reflect—the world a blur with little meaning and emotion. And, foolishly believing that no one ever needs to relearn how to walk.

During your recovery, we sought signs of success. The first assisted step, then one by yourself. A stroll down a hall, with no handrail! Up an incline, around the room. You hesitated at the stairs, raising a foot then missing the step—suddenly a new barrier, unfamiliar territory, a new skill to learn.

But the real breakthrough came later. In life, not all things are level and smooth. There are no sidewalks out on the farm, and you had to learn how to walk on uneven ground.

Reevaluate your progress. Even the therapists were surprised by our request, our demand. You needed to find out: could you handle irregular surfaces, learn to feel more with your soles, combine sight and touch so they worked in tandem, responding to the irregular terrain? You had to discover where you were.

At first we had difficulty even finding dirt. The hospital grounds were manicured; evenly mowed grass with a few smoothly raked spots of brown soil; even irrigation lines buried and seamless. But if you wanted to get back to work, you'd have to navigate the roughest territory: soft and hard earth, rocks and dirt clods, rises and dips, shadows hiding divots and holes. Toss in some vine clippings and tree branches, and mud and dust with big clumps of weeds—yes, don't forget the weeds—just like home. Your goal became "to go home." Overcome fears, more failure than success. You had already conquered flat surfaces, but did you have the will to face another challenge? And is "conquer" the right term, as if this were a battle? You'd never be the same. We can't fix your brain and simply remove the blood clot. Engaging in a war implies winners and losers, as if it were a game. This was work, some days better than others. Celebrate little things, accept setbacks. The process would never be done. Like farming, more trees and vines to prune, water, and fertilize, and there's always another harvest to pick. A Zen Buddhist phrase comes to mind: "The pot is always boiling." There will always be more uneven ground.

As we challenged you to work more, I kept thinking about being realistic: when would we reach the acceptance stage of recovery, satisfied with what we have? The solution wasn't to lower expectations, but to create different expectations. Take one step at a time, then just one more step. Reinvent yourself because you are now different.

Modern medicine celebrates when it can fix things and that's truly amazing. Hearts can be repaired, the process much more mechanical, fitting well the evolution of technology and science into medical practices. Pills, procedures, inventions—all designed to fix. Healing reduced to technology.

But Dad, after your stroke, you couldn't be fixed. No pill reversed the damage. Recovery would be neither fun nor simple. You were cheated out of a part of your life, dealt a lousy hand of cards. Allow yourself a few moments of self-pity, then back out to practice. Learn to walk as best you can.

Now, I can see myself as I age—a few more twists and sprains and sore muscles and back pain. I think we'd all be better off, become better people, if we had to relearn the little but important things and accept the diverse terrains we have to negotiate. A metaphor for all of us: learning how to walk on uneven ground.

Your son,
Mas

Slow Trucks

Dear Mr. Hatayama,

    You drove a slow pick-up truck. I remember you in your old, bright orange Dodge puttering down our country roads, taking your time. You and the truck, a used County of Fresno vehicle, took your time. You seemed oblivious to the world behind you, enjoying a leisurely ride past your neighbors' farms.

    Happy to go slow, your truck wanted to chug along, content in first or second gear instead of overdrive. Lounging at a top speed of ten miles an hour, you eased down the avenues, lingered at stop signs. I bet you could count the white lines as they passed beneath your vehicle.

    Once in a while, I found myself driving behind your slow truck. I'd grow anxious and begin to wonder: "Why is that old man going so slow? What's the matter with that driver?" (As if the problem was with you and not me.) Sometimes, I dangerously passed you, impatience overruling logic, rushing to get to the next stop sign a few seconds ahead.

    But I can recall that while pulling even with your truck I'd glance over and see your face. You were calm and relaxed. Not necessarily smiling but certainly driving with a look of contentment. I believe you were lost in thoughts, simply thinking. You seemed satisfied to go slow.

We, too, had our own slow trucks. Actually, we had three. A '74 Ford Courier that sits in my dad's yard where I parked it years ago when I finally got a replacement in the early nineties. It still sits more or less in the same area.

Things sit a lot out on farms. Actually, I think old trucks like to sit a while. They pretend to be aging like fine wine.

Another truck rests in my dad's shed, a '72 Chevy that he last drove in 1989. He couldn't start it one winter morning and simply left it there. It still sits—and he uses the cab as his office, storing papers and tractor repair manuals out of the weather. Don't ask why, but once in a while I even check the air pressure in those tires, I suppose just to make sure it's still all right.

My truck was a Mitsubishi that I purchased new in 1991. Fifteen years later, it had only twelve thousand miles on it. I rarely drove it into town. Most trips were back and forth between our farmhouse and my folks, about a quarter-mile away. I'd make that trip two or three times a day. I once calculated that to be about a thousand times a year, perhaps ten thousand times over the truck's lifetime—or about four thousand miles.

That truck drove down our dusty farm avenues and trails and through peach orchards, barely clearing low-hanging branches. (Not always, though. A few very low branches, you might say, were "pruned" by the top of the truck cab.) Over the years, miles added up as I hauled boxes, carried peaches, distributed bundles of raisin trays.

When I told Marcy, my wife, the truck only had twelve thousand miles, she said that was incorrect.

I pleaded, "Really, go check the odometer and see for yourself."

Her response: "No, that's wrong. You back up a lot."

I paused and conceded she was right, I do back up frequently. Some of our avenues don't have a way out, the only thing you can do is to put the truck in reverse to get out. Driving into an orchard, unless you go past the halfway point, it makes more sense to back out to get back onto the avenue.

A lot of times, like when checking water, I'd drive a little forward to see where the water had reached in the rows, then back up to double-check or recount the rows, to make sure I had the right ones, so when I adjusted the irrigation valves at the other end of the field, I would shut the proper ones.

And sometimes, it's just more fun to drive backwards; too much trouble to turn around. I've mastered the art of driving in reverse, fairly quickly, trusting only my mirrors. Heading backwards may feel fast but it's really not. After all, these are pick-up trucks that like to go slow, real slow. Right, Mr. Hatayama?

Your disposition matched a few other characters in our community who also drove slow. "Old man Flint" eased down Jefferson Avenue in his equally distinctive tan Studebaker Lark. Though it was not a truck, he still used it for farm chores and often tossed a shovel in the back seat, the handle sticking out of the rear window. His old farm car seemed to last for decades. Then I realized that when one wore out, he simply got another just like it, even the same color.

"Old Mister Steele," another neighbor, also drove slow with a major difference. He cruised along in a green Chrysler Imperial. The car seemed to float by our place, gliding down the road on a daily trip to Del Rey. He even got his hair cut once a week "in town."

Yet Mr. Steele shared something in common with you, Mr. Hatayama. You both drove slow while smoking a cigar.

The cigar fit you—part of the image of someone relaxing, savoring the flavors of life. I can instantly recall your classic pose: a straw farmer hat pushed back above the forehead, allowing a cool summer breeze to ease into the cab and across your face. You drove with one hand, the other holding the stogie. Your left elbow stuck out of the open window (and who drives anymore with their window open?), the rest of the arm relaxing on the door frame. I could never figure out why the cigar didn't burn out faster with that pose until I realized just how slow you were driving. Just the right speed to keep the cigar lit, yet it could last for hours.

Mr. Hatayama, you seemed to want to teach the world a lesson. You and your slow truck wanted to mosey along, take your time. Life is fast enough, certainly there are times during the workday to go slow.

I, too, try to drive slow, at least sometimes. I tease

myself with the thought, I'm much too important to rush. "No sweat," I say out loud, grinning. When I putter along, for a few moments the hard-working farmer can rest. I can show the world I'm rich, not with money or respect but with time.

Go slow.

Your neighbor,
Mas Masumoto

Culture of Fog

Dear Kenji,

As a transplant from outside the Central Valley, now working at the University of California, Merced, you are spending one of your first winters here. Like this institution, you plan to stay here a while. But because you are new to the Valley, I'm not sure you understand the culture of fog.

Fog: a cloud on the ground formed when humid air is cooled, causing water vapor to condense into tiny drops. The moisture hovers in the stationary air, locked in a holding pattern until outside winds push out the cold air or the sun heats the ground enough so the moisture "burns off." Heed my warning, Kenji: there will be days when the fog is so thick you can't see beyond a few feet in front of you and there may be times when the sun hides for weeks.

Fog: treacherous, dangerous, a cold, unforgiving character that tricks newcomers. People drive too fast; traffic accidents blanket the countryside; fresh skid marks are painted daily; and cars and trucks pile up with fatalities. We're forced to adapt to the curse of going slow, a pace that doesn't seem to fit with the larger world.

Schools still mind the weather in the Valley. Foggy-day schedules delay the start of school, some kids (and a few teachers) cheer while bus drivers groan. We're compelled to accept nature's timeline, a piece of our rural past not to be dismissed.

Peaches and nectarines need this winter cold. Fog helps keep temperatures below 45 degrees and the "chilling hours" necessary for trees to slip into a deserved dormancy and awaken renewed. And why not farmers? I'm convinced the American work pace, with little time for vacation, is unnatural and unhealthy. Fog helps remind me that down time, extended morning breaks, even naps and respites, are not necessarily evil signs of weakness.

Fog remains a test for new arrivals. They love it or hate it. The blistering heat of summer and the bone-chilling fog create a world of absolutes: hot or cold—accept us or leave us—with seemingly little tolerance of anything in between. Our fog contains a hardness, reflecting a disconnect with the rest of the state. Outsiders believe we in the Valley are lost in the fog. (Have you heard a similar whisper when you told others about your relocation to UC Merced?) Meanwhile, Valley natives seem to enjoy the isolation and separation from those living along the "left coast."

Fog arrives as early as November and sticks around until February. Visitors swear at the fog, proclaiming this is why our valley is a place to bypass. Even our residents have few romantic images of cool, misty evenings with diffused city streetlights beckoning intrigue. (Although I have been tempted to write about the mysterious luster of a lonely country farmhouse and barnyard light glowing in the late-night fog, beginning my great American novel with the line "It was a dark and foggy night...")

But Kenji, I trust you're learning to work in the fog. I sense you understand how farmers can trudge into hazy fields in winter and lose themselves in a wondrous world. Robbed of sight, the other senses are heightened. The hum of traffic can be heard in the distance, barking dogs warn of strangers, even birds continue their songs in winter. Listen to the moisture drip, drip, drip from leaves like a natural timepiece, a perfect slow pace to work while reflecting. Forced to use other senses, we find the surrounding world stirs with new life.

I recall one Christmas day when my grandmother journeyed out to prune vines, a seventy-year-old bundled up to snip, clip, and slice in the fog. I located her by listening to the snapping of grapevine canes accompanied by the screech of trellis wires. Hidden in the fog, she seemed content in her work, a moment of peace in her adopted land, even during that holiday.

Fog reminds me that this is a land of work, places where people still value productivity and hand labor matters; we're still blue-collar and real. Hard, honest work speaks about our character as we labor in the fog.

Perhaps we need an initiation ceremony for newcomers, exposing them to the traditions of fog—how to drive in it, how to work in it, how to maintain your sanity when you don't see the sun for hours and days. (The first winter my wife, Marcy, came to the Valley, she didn't see the sun for fifteen days and grew restless, almost depressed. Her moods matched the gray sky. It was a test of love, I suppose, for she chose to stay.)

My initiation program will reveal stages of acceptance. First, the recognition of the wet chill wrapping its cold fingers around you. The Valley: dense and damp, robbing you of the sense of sight, a symbol for a lack of vision? Then will come another side, trusting your other senses and an odd sense of security, a feeling of solitude while working in the fog. Perhaps fog protects us from outsiders and allows us time to ponder while life slows down.

I've heard of leadership retreats with participants hiking at night without light; the personal training of leaders as they maneuver through uncharted territory, trusting their senses, listening to instincts, separating the fools from the thinkers, distinguishing the overly cautious or wild from those with the wisdom to slow down and think.

Can't our relationship with fog be a metaphor for development in the Valley, our fields of practice for smart growth and sustainable planning? Perhaps it's okay to slow down in the race to develop our lands instead of communities rear-ending each other and creating massive traffic jams. Can we move forward steadily but paced?

I hope we one day create our own culture of fog, with legends of our spirit and songs to celebrate our beliefs. Perhaps even a fog festival? (Yet skeptics would comment, "How can you interact if you can't see each other?") For the moment, our stories may be hidden, a secret even to those who live here. One day though, I imagine UC Merced, Fresno State, and our other institutions of learning rising out of the Valley's fog. While we may be invisible in the fog of winter, we're working to prepare for spring.

I'll take my stand in the fog. This is who we are, part of the story of the Valley. As for those in the rest of the state who disdain our culture, perhaps they are the ones lost in the fog.

Your friend,
Mas

The Wave and Head Nod

Dear Dad,

You taught me how to wave when we worked in the fields. The arm is raised slowly, allowing for recognition despite the distance. A dramatic reaching for the sky, a single hand stretches upwards, fingers open. Hold it upright until seen and greeted with a like response, the space between two shrinking with each second. Then turn to separate fields for another pass down a row, workers disappearing back into the landscape.

Over a field, across an irrigation ditch, opposite sides of a dirt avenue, a wave becomes the common language of place. The wave, a moment of recognition between two individuals, each saying, "You matter."

I've tried this wave in big cities and have failed miserably. Perhaps people were moving too fast or they traveled at a pace that encourages anonymity. It's easier to maneuver if you look past faceless bodies. In the bubble of city life, few looked up from their urban drive. Their stares focusing straight forward, they were travelers intent on reaching their destinations.

Studies like the classic *The Lonely Crowd* or *Bowling Alone* warned me: waving in the city doesn't often work. I could have been invisible. Actually, once in a big city I was noticed or at least misinterpreted. Someone responded to my wave with a middle-finger wave back at me.

But I still expect a wave back. I grew up working outdoors and using my hands. Accompanied by a slow, rural pace, the act of waving becomes second nature. I know that a genuine wave, like a solid handshake, can overcome many differences. Here in our valley, I most often wave to non-English speakers. Our lack of a common language matters little. We are joined by a working-class bond.

There are cultural variations of waving. Asians may wave but most will perform the head dip, as if bowing from the neck up. This act corresponds with the common practice of not looking at others in the eyes.

Sometimes this sort of greeting can become dangerous. In Japanese culture, the lower the bow, the more respectful. Once, I saw two Asians meet while driving. The younger one, showing the utmost social graces, tried to deeply dip his head and bonged it on the steering wheel. Fortunately they were both driving slowly.

Latinos wave, but more often (and this is true with many men) they just do a head nod. It can be very subtle. You have to be looking for it. The chin is slightly pushed upward as a sign of recognition. Even simpler, sometimes only the eyebrows and forehead are raised. If I hesitate, I'll miss the opportunity to return the gesture. It requires an understanding of cultural expectations that I have yet to master: exactly when does one raise the eyebrows or nod the head or wave with the hand?

Does gender make a difference? My sense is that men wave more than women do. Does it have to do with how a woman's wave may be misconstrued? Are there other subgroups and cultural differences? Do gays wave more than others, or is there a gay man wave? Do second-generation immigrant families in America wave more or less than foreign-born parents?

Dad, all this matters because waving is an act of public recognition. We acknowledge each other with a wave, a visible sign proclaiming that the other exists. I find that comforting, something that builds community and creates neighbors. Go to a place where people don't care for each other, I doubt if you see waves or head nods.

I know I sound old, but I am struck by the role of technology in relation to waves or head nods, especially with the youth culture and the proliferation of cell phones and iPods. People can't wave when focused on a cell phone call. Hooked to an iPod, listeners check out, oblivious to the world around them, escaping into the loud music and that's the point.

Individuals remain individuals once they insulate themselves with their headsets and music. They create zones of distance, barriers to the outside, public signs to keep others away.

I believe we're losing the art of physically communicating. In a high-tech world, the wave or head nod gives way to a text message or becomes ignored and lost amidst two hundred downloads. A digital revolution requires less reading of body language and more scanning of e-mails and blogs. People pay less attention to the immediate physical world and focus more attention on the virtual world.

So what? Is my wave relegated to a dying, old world culture, my head nod or bow a remnant of traditions that no longer have a place? Or is it just a matter of aging? With maturity, I have discovered the need for more waves and nods (I include hugs too—even more "man hugs"). I do know that old folks, because of their declining eyesight and hearing, rely more and more on touch. Waves, handshakes, and hugs mean a lot.

So thanks, Dad, for teaching me how to wave. I will continue to test my theories, even on the youth. I'll wave and wait for a response. At first, I may get an odd reaction, the other person thinking, "Am I supposed to know you?" Those that are uncomfortable will ignore me.

I trust the majority will smile once they get past "What's the matter with that guy who keeps waving at me?"

Nothing's the matter. Just wave back.

Unwaveringly,
Your son

PART FIVE

Stories

Leaving Behind Stories

Dear Children,

When I die, what will I leave behind for you?

The things I cherish most are stories and memories that matter. I cherish things we've done as family and with friends, places and people and events that linger: breakfast on the farmhouse porch or a warm, late-afternoon farm walk and talk, sharing the first ripe peach of the season, the juices running down your face. Rich in details, characters with depth, authentic emotions— memories that come alive when embedded in the context of story. That's how I hope to leave my legacy.

What will forever be a part of my story? The land and farm. The greatest memorial to our family will be the farmland that stays behind, something you can touch and feel and smell. Something I can share with family and friends, neighbors and community.

Is our farm the story of great achievements? Has our business grown and expanded with huge profits? Not really. As I've grown older, I've come to realize it's not success I hope to leave behind. Rather, it's significance.

And how do I measure this? My worth is defined by

the stories bound to the land and that's why I hope we can keep working the fields. To be blunt, I didn't farm so my heirs could make a fortune in a land deal. I don't believe that's what you want, either.

Do all family farmers think this way? No. Yet I dream of a few bold farmers who will draw the line in the dirt, leave behind a farm and be forever remembered as people who loved and worked the earth. That's their simple story of significance. Imagine forever altering the landscape by keeping it the same: a farm that retains its identity while a region holds onto a piece of its history. To know who we are because we still have a sense of where we are.

I've seen other places radically change in a generation. Santa Clara County, once called the "Valley of Heart's Delight," boasted miles and miles of orchards brimming with apricots and prunes. Decades ago, Blossom Hill Road had meaning in spring, in a region filled with blooming fruit trees. Today, all the towns are connected by houses and freeways, seemingly the same urban sprawl repeated over and over as if memories of the old no longer matter. Must our Valley towns become anonymous because they no longer have borders of identity? Can't we still grow but not grow into each other with only a city limit sign identifying where one place ends and another begins?

Is this important or am I just getting old, swelling with nostalgia? I accept change and growth, I do not dream of returning to the 1950s, when a majority of us in the Valley lived on family farms. Instead, I simply want to keep some farms to show where food is grown and to remember places that still matter. Future generations may want to see and feel that story and know where their daily nourishment comes from.

Open spaces have a magical quality. Imagine for a moment standing in the sunshine and breathing in the air; see the green of nature and smell the freshness of spring or ripeness of summer; long to taste something real and honest. Touch a distant memory and recall a farm family's history: many Valley families are rooted in a place with dirt under our souls. A family farm, not much different than an old growth forest or historical site: a sacred place, a voice shouting that we count, we matter.

Children, I'm not worried about whether you farm; I sense someone will still plant something. It's part of what many long to do. No one says all farms and farmers have to go away, a victim of changing economics. Perhaps new immigrants, following in your great-grandparents' footsteps, will rent the farm as a stepping stone to planting roots in American soil. These farms can then supply local and regional farmer's markets, connecting the land to a city population.

As cities grow, planners too recognize the value of farmlands and open spaces. The view of the landscape and the feel define a city just as much as its neighborhoods and housing developments. As an urban farm, consider community gardens and walking trails, a return to the wild and the openness of our valley with native grasses and wildlife. Imagine if they had done that in other urban areas a generation ago. It doesn't take much, as just one strategic farm can become a grand regional park.

Even a few farming neighbors can join together to create a greenbelt. By keeping farms, we redirect city growth away from prime farmland and possibly protect a region, or at least delay the march of houses, buying time for regions to plan and communities to redefine what they want. Farmers then leave behind a statement: this is who we were and can still be. Many of us in agriculture do protect the environment and we need to remind city folks that good farmers are stewards. We look after the countryside because we have ownership.

Perhaps it's just a matter of families asking themselves "Do we want to keep the farm?" Children, our farm is still miles from the city, but in your lifetime, change will happen. So why do I share my story now? So you'll be able to answer the question "What would Dad have wanted?"

I hope you save and mail this letter to all the family, so they too can hear the need for stories that contribute to memory and legacy. Families talk too much about leaving the right things behind, yet few actually make a commitment. This will be a family decision not always spelled out in a will. It's about having the will, a crusade to save things that matter: "grounded stories" that make the difference between success and significance. It may mean the difference between lots of money or something else and I vote for something else.

Farm memories are buried in the land, and dreams live in these fields. I hope you share my cause: to romance the next farm generation. There's something important here, just the way we are. It's activism in the fields: Be radical and grow food, raise a family out in the country, and keep something right.

So my children, I'll need your help to leave behind a memory and keep alive a story of significance.

Your dad

Ofuro (Japanese Bath)

Dear *Baachan* (Grandma),

I visited with you last night as the family took their bath in an *ofuro*—a Japanese bath.

Although you passed away, I still remember when I was a child and you helped me take a bath. Forty years ago, we had an old-style ofuro, modeled after those in Japan. Immigrants constructed a large metal box that held water and was heated by a fire. Your job was to make and tend the fire for the entire family. We initially washed by squatting outside of the tub, using the hot water to rinse, then easing into the steaming water to soak. We took turns, the kids first, then Mom and Dad, and you last. The entire family shared the same water.

The ofuro, a tradition Japanese brought from the homeland: a personal ritual of cleansing, a communal act of family. Quite differently than the "once a week on Saturday night" practice in rural America, Baachan, you tried to bathe daily. Closing your eyes, heat rising around you, for a moment did you return to your Japanese village, no longer an alien in a strange land?

Did other immigrants to this valley bring their cleansing

customs with them? The personal, often private traditions of a family that carried the meaning of culture; an almost forgotten act because it was a simple part of daily life.

❦

Recently in a junk pile, I found an old ofuro from your time, cleaned it, and patched a slight leak. We then reenacted the Japanese American tradition. The galvanized metal box, only twenty-eight inches wide, three feet long, and two feet deep, felt so very familiar; just the right size for small people; curled up, I could easily fit. The top edges were rolled over and rounded, gentle as the flesh

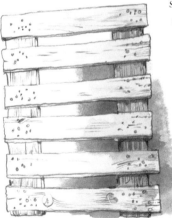

slid across the surface when we slipped into the simmering liquid. Like you, earlier in the evening I had made a fire to heat the water. Fueled by old redwood stakes and grapevines, the fire burned brightly, smoke curling around the metal tub, threatening to ignite the raisin-sweatbox stand I had set to the side as a washing station.

I bathed with my son Korio, your great-grandson. Scooping water with a small wooden bucket, we could smell the scent of pine as the water cascaded over our heads. It splashed on the sweatbox, the sound of water dripping as we stood naked, a cool summer breeze tickling our backs in sudden contrast to the hot water. Again we rinsed ourselves, shivering as the evening air descended on our skin with a gentle tickle.

We slid into the heated water, which was initially almost too hot. As our skin adjusted to the temperature, we squatted, then sat as the water rose across our chests, up to our chins. The world seemed to slow down, the sunset gone, the last light of the day passing into night. Water dripped into the fire and hissed, a wisp of smoke wandered upward, a cleansing smell with the ofuro.

We took a family bath in perhaps the only ofuro left on an American farm. Sharing the waters of history, a Japanese American baptism. Will many from a new generation take an ofuro with the smoke, hot water, and quiet rituals? Could we perhaps make it inviting by renaming it the "original California hot tub"?

❧

I told Kori the story about Japanese immigrants watching the sun set, knowing it was descending on their native lands across an ocean. But Baachan, you and others may have thought differently, you came to America to create a homeland. Assimilate and become American, but also respect traditions, like an ofuro. Immigrants need not abandon the old. They could honor the cultural baggage they carried over a border, across an ocean; a part of their past that was important enough to recreate and retain.

Few immigrants could afford to import the cast iron baths from Japan and perhaps you never wanted to. Instead you adapted your baths, using galvanized sheet metal and rivets to hold the corner pieces—strong enough to last for decades.

I imagine the first baths were open-air tubs that sat atop hardpan rocks, a fire beneath them. They were located away from the farmhouse, reducing the risk of accidental fire and offering some privacy. Later, a cement slab was poured for proper drainage away from the fire. I remember most families built a small wooden shack, a *furoba*, to keep out the weather with some privacy (although I do recall, as a curious child, peeking through the cracks in the wood siding).

My mom tells the story of when she had to make the fire—the job of the youngest child because parents and older siblings were working long hours in the fields. Experienced fire builders knew how to quickly make embers to heat the water slowly and evenly. Instead, Mom made a roaring fire and the furoba ignited. She rarely had fire duty again.

I was most intrigued by the ofuro's wooden raft. Since water was heated directly by a fire, the bottom of the tub grew very hot, so a wooden raft was built to keep your feet and bottom from touching it. Over the years, the water-soaked wood grew loose and more nails were added; the raft must now have over a hundred nails, a timeline of the generations of use.

As a child, I was always terrified that somehow the raft would topple and I'd burn my feet. Since I was too light to sink the raft into the water, it was tradition that all the kids took their ofuro together, the only way to combine enough weight for the wood to sink to the bottom so our young bodies could soak. We three siblings played games, threatening to jump out and destroy the balance or pretending to be in a stormy ocean that rocked and created waves, splashing water out of the ofuro and wasting hot water. I can still hear your voice, Baachan, scolding us kids with a low but shrill "ahhhh," smiling as you shook your head.

Later as an exchange student to Japan, I lived in the small village you emigrated from and took an ofuro in the same metal tub you bathed in as a child. Every evening we built a fire, washed, and soaked, sharing the water. We relaxed, we told stories. I learned about family, farming rice, the history of the ancient farmhouse. Baachan, even your stoic brother, who took over the family rice farm, became conversational during the ofuro. This was a place for stories and creating stories.

Your grandson,
Dave Mas

Ben's Revolution

Dear Ben,

The revolution will not be televised. I believe you already know this as you cover news about the Valley's Southeast Asian community. You are among the few Southeast Asian journalists, part of a new media of a new valley, and, though you may not call yourself this, one of the new revolutionaries.

There is a revolution of change here as immigrant populations arrive to a new land with their own languages, beliefs, and traditions. But this valley is not an open frontier with unsettled territory and vast spaces. We are an old land with old people and old communities already established. A pioneer generation of a hundred years ago could settle here; the new community of pioneers arrives and changes things.

When my grandparents immigrated to the Valley from Japan in 1898 and 1918, the divide wasn't as wide. Most everything was new. Borders were still being drawn. The class schism wasn't as pronounced. Settlers could settle without displacing or replacing. Like most immigrants, they arrived with dreams of a better life.

Yet today it seems different, as if immigrants start

further behind and their dream is simply to catch up. The poor hope to become middle class. Ethnic communities strive to become American without a common mythology; I don't hear anyone talking about the melting-pot theory anymore. Immigrants plant roots so that the next generation becomes native to a place. I'm not so sure that my grandparents, who feared returning to their homelands as failures, were as confident as the new immigrants.

But Ben, you and my ancestors share something: rarely are you seen. Nothing new to America, a history of the visible and invisible, a repeated story of struggle as immigrants arrive as weeds and, if fortunate, find a niche in our lands and survive. Do you dream of one day becoming a native grass? I wonder if under our skin we Asians and people of color are still perceived as weeds as we wear our faces.

Today, the public has heard a repeated immigrant's tale and seemingly has lost interest. In this age of entertainment media, only the negative stories of change make the news. A restless, mass-media audience is hungry for the exceptional, curious for the eccentric. The superficial-yet-peculiar draws attention. But we are only understood by stories, not sound bites, and every community needs a storyteller. That's what you are, Ben, that's your revolution.

Stories help place experience in the context of history. Instead of isolated events, the waves of immigrants continue to change the face of America, especially California. (For Native Americans, their history is about immigrants arriving to forever change their lands.) Stories create full characters, not paper-thin and flat caricatures.

Immigrants arrive as individuals, families, and communities, carrying their baggage of tradition and culture to leave an imprint on a new land. Stories allow lives to be told, the how and why and not just the when and where of history. People exposed to stories can elevate their understanding of the whole, instead of basing their judgment on a few bits and pieces of information and innuendo. Stories help legitimize experience.

But stories and current trends in broadcast media are often in conflict: stories take time to be told and are often slow-paced. Contrast that to television and cable news and the demand for more and more speed; being first seems more important than being right. Speed can kill stories.

The challenge you face, Ben, may be that you have to do both, working with the speed of today's media and staying aware of the power of story. Is that any different than the pioneer's challenge: to be stronger and smarter, armed with a passion and drive to live the dream of the immigrant?

Ironically, you can take comfort in knowing that people of color are too often invisible, our voices frequently muted by others and quiet; our stories neglected. We don't have to prop up characters in order to display instant heroes and leaders—the public isn't clamoring for a good read. No need to fabricate an acceptable yet captivating story line as if we star in a reality TV show. We can create our own mythologies naturally and over time. No rush to stampede our story's conclusion because few are really listening. Does the general public worry about how Southeast Asians work in America? Or does the latest celebrity trial or sports scandal steal headlines?

Ben, you and others tell the stories of our communities of color: quiet to the outside world, our tales echo with an authentic language from a place invisible to most. Our voices can be lost except for the whisper of ethnic media.

If I pause, I can hear it when I scan the radio and hear a foreign tongue. I'm stunned, unable to decipher what language is spoken. Or see a glimpse on TV as I flip through channels and spy brighter color schemes, lively with a different spirit. Or pick up a piece of paper and become illiterate; the lines and marks not only foreign but making me feel alien. Could this be California? Yes.

Ethnic media works when it tells stories with a point of view from community, sharing the insider's voice. They can become great when experiences are placed in context: to see a people's history as part of something larger. Ben, we're forever part of the "Other California," and we survive as both weeds and natural grasses. That's when we understand that the revolution will not be televised.

Your new friend,
Mas

The Story Economy

Dear *Baachan* (Grandma),

I remember watching you eat the perfect peach. You'd close your eyes, breathe in the aroma, and slip a juicy slice past your lips. With first bite, the nectar exploded and flavor drenched your taste buds. A satisfied glow gently spread across your face. A moment of savoring; soothing, content, perfection.

I believe the flavors transported you—memories of peaches in Japan as a child; working a lifetime in the orchards of California; building an industry as a farmworker. Now your memories have become part of our family farm and the work we do.

I'm driven by these haunting memories. Not just of the flavor of a peach but the stories of how they're grown and who grows them. Beyond lifeless commodities, human relationships lie at the core of great produce, adding to the flavors we enjoy. I call it the "story economy." It journeys with wonderful foods: powerful, intimate, personal narratives about food; insight into the faces behind our meals. I also think it's how our businesses and communities need to be developed.

The story economy incorporates the power of memory and traditions. Not nostalgia for the "good old days" that can no longer be (and for some never were that great). Rather, I refer to work that takes the best from the past as motivation to build and invest in a better future.

Think of the new significance placed on taste and flavor in the exclusive organic marketplace. Baachan, could you have imagined our peaches in gourmet restaurants or becoming the prized centerpiece of an evening dinner? We've become part of the new California cuisine that emphasizes fresh, local, and in-season food. It's the link of people with a place, and the story becomes part of a summer meal.

Think of the growing success of community-supported agriculture, where consumers become direct subscribers and supporters of farmers by ordering a share of weekly harvests. The stories of foods evolve into personal relationships between consumer and farmer.

Think of the revival of farmer's markets throughout the state that bring farmers and communities together. Often placed in downtowns, these gatherings help connect people and serve to revitalize an area. (I also think of the stories about baseball and downtown stadiums that work in a similar fashion.) The blend of flavor and people combines with the feel of a real place, a neighborhood, a city center; something authentic is created and enjoyed.

I value stories that go beyond economic and monetary relationships. A search for that perfect memory adds meaning to my life's work, a quest for that tale I'm proud to pass down to generations.

Of course, not all products and places work in the

story economy. I'm not sure we have much memory of mass-produced goods such as fast foods, which people consume but can't recall a few minutes later. Commuters pass through nameless places because they don't need to remember them; they're oblivious that such neighborhoods may be home to others who remain faceless. People pay for entertainment that blurs together so one action movie or reality TV show more or less looks like another. Consumers take comfort in not being challenged; passive entertainment works for lazy thinkers. Most will forget these anonymous moments when they don't attach significance.

Baachan, your perfect peach story works because it's authentic. I employ all my senses: I can see the harvest glow in a peach with early morning light and feel the soft flesh; I breathe in the aroma while salivating as I think about the flavor; I anticipate hearing the smacking of lips over and over after each bite.

By thinking in stories, I'm forced to slow down and reflect, attaching words to the moment and committing feelings to memory. The story economy works because I can use these terms to help recall the experience later and relive something pleasurable. Advertising tries to do this but it's not the same: these are my expressions for my remembrances of things past.

I fear we're losing stories because we choose not to remember; we forget too quickly and too easily. This is how great-tasting peaches are lost—farming in a system that regrettably rewards great-looking fruits. As if at the point of sale, only what's outside matters, with little consideration and memory of what's good inside.

Responsibility comes with remembering. It requires work, it burdens us with thought. If we don't care about the future, it's simple to overlook stupid decisions in the present. Consider the sprawl of our Valley cities: poor planning decisions are now too easily forgotten and forgiven, no one willing to take ownership of how our valley will look twenty years from now. We need to organize city summits and community forums to plan and claim our futures.

Historical amnesia may be the greatest threat to our stories. If we forget our quest for things good, we forego things that will be great.

Vision comes from our ability to look to the future because we value stories of the past. I honor all the Valley's flavors. I respect what we are, not what we are not: from blossom trails to fresh fruit roadstands to folk artists and Valley poets; from immigrants arriving with their traditions and festivals to the swap meets and flea markets that speak to our own culture.

I think we need to have an annual Highway 99 swap meet festival to celebrate the stories found in people's stuff; the gems and junk from our attics and garages, up and down the Valley; our own brand of cultural tourism as our stories go public.

Yet, some of our stories remain incomplete, the rest

of the state ignoring our valley and its people. Some, for example, call our need for a University of California campus a "boondoggle," questioning why would "you folks" need such an institution of higher learning? Their thinking: we're just a colony, part of the other California, exporting the brightest youth from our lands to boarding schools where they supposedly can be provided with the proper stories of California. We're denied access to our culture because our stories are deemed worthless.

Baachan, your story helps make this farm a home. We shared a peach memory that continues to motivate today. I, too, close my eyes as I eat a great peach. I can see and hear and feel you and the stories continue to live. Perfection for generations. Priceless.

Your grandson,
Mas

Farewell Letters

Dear Reader,

Have you ever written a final letter? A letter of resignation? Did you ever write or receive what used to be called a "Dear John" letter, an announcement of a breakup, a dissolving of a relationship? Have you read a final letter to or from a family member near the end of life? What would go in such a letter, what final thoughts would someone want to share?

An older generation used letters very differently. During World War II, soldiers understood the value of "mail call," a time when letters from home caught up with a company, a moment when a word from family and friends back in the States meant a lot. Soldiers wrote back, sharing thoughts, emotions, fears, or simply using writing as a break from the war and fighting. People clung to letters as a touchstone to their homes, a conduit to reach out and be with family.

Letters also carried tragic news. My grandmother kept the letter from a chaplain informing her that her son had been killed in action during World War II; a letter she could not read because she was illiterate, yet she still kept safely tucked away.

I know of a letter written to a soldier by his fiancée, who called off the engagement. He was in Europe fighting Germans; she had a change of heart back in America and had to be honest with him. Can you imagine how that letter was received? Imagine how hard it was to write that letter.

Letter writing is slow and forces you to commit your thoughts to words. Written words are revealing; they capture self-expression much differently than a conversation. No one writes in a letter, "Oh, I didn't mean what I just wrote" or "I take that back, I wasn't thinking when I wrote that."

You think, then you write.

(Although I have read e-mails that defy my thinking—people proving that they can write without thinking and somehow push "send" instead of "delete.")

Letters demand reflection because they can be read over and over, even passed around and shared with others. Once they are sent, thoughts and feelings can't be easily erased.

Of course, there are modern alternatives for communication. Clearly the telephone allows the human voice to be heard and carries vocal intonation. But more often, even when we are armed with cell phones, busy schedules conflict with answering a phone. The answering machine then becomes the convenient messenger.

This is especially true in cases (and I must admit, at times I too have been guilty of this) where the caller phones and hopes no one answers. Declining an invitation, making weak excuses for tardiness, even breaking up a relationship—all based on a faulty premise that one-way messages are communication. I've fooled myself at times into believing my words were well received.

An extension of the phone, sanctioned by today's youth culture, is the text message. Like modern-day Morse code, the art of this communication lies in using the fewest letters and words to convey an idea. I suppose it's good that people are still writing and perhaps the brevity of text messages can acquire even more meaning, like a modern form of abbreviated poetry. But it's the immediacy that matters more than anything else does: to send the message exactly the moment you feel it. Speed counts, not content.

My daughter, Nikiko, shared a story: a friend of hers witnessed the breakup of a boyfriend and girlfriend via a text message war. The two parties furiously sent messages back and forth. Emotions reigned— not necessarily expressed in the language but rather in the frantic pushing of the telephone's number pads—racing to respond in a duel, to see who could send the shortest and quickest blunt rebuttal and get in the final word.

Here are the final moments of that text message conversation.

Screen message: "It's over."

Rapid-fire return: "FINE."

The final word: "FINE."

(Number pad sequence: #3 push, push, push; #4 push, push, push; #6 stab, stab; #3 stab, stab; Send button: punch hard and long, with emotion.)

That's why I write. I want to leave behind letters that use whole sentences and paragraphs with meaning and significance. If I'm lucky, my stories are read and reread.

I mean what I write. I live with the haunting thought that my words can stay with the reader for a while and may remain with me forever. That's what I hope for. Not required: punching the Send button hard.

Thanks,
Mas Masumoto

Author Acknowledgments

I do not write alone. Many inspire, help, and support my passion.

Thanks to those at the *Fresno Bee*, including my former editor Charlie Waters as well as publisher Ray Steele, executive editor Betsy Lumbye, editor Jim Boren, and many others, who contribute to each column with a personal touch. Also many thanks to Doug Hansen—his artwork elevates every column and I'm pleased to do another book with him.

Working with Heyday Books continues to be a joy. Thanks to Malcolm Margolin, Jeannine Gendar, Gayle Wattawa, Lorraine Rath, Diane Lee, and Patricia Wakida.

I'm grateful for neighbors, friends, and family who allow me to write letters to them, including Bob Flint and the Scouts of Del Rey's Troop 87. Also thanks to the many whose "first names" grace my letters—Fred Ruiz, Ben Vue, Dan Farnesi, Kenji Hakuta, Jim Tucker, John Gray, Mr. Hatayama, Fresno's weather forecasters, and Alice Waters.

In addition, I want to acknowledge my wife, Marcy, who tolerates many conversations about every essay, story, and letter. Her willingness to listen to each idea, no matter how uninformed it sounds, provides essential support. Perhaps that's why she needed to get her doctorate in education following decades of our daily seminars, convoluted conversations, and occasional lectures.

And thanks to my children, Nikiko and Korio. Both inspire and challenge me. They do their best to keep me young while making me old.

Finally, thanks to all those who read and enjoy listening to a good story. You keep me believing in great things—on the farm and in my stories.

—David Mas Masumoto

Illustrator Acknowledgments

My fruitful collaboration with David "Mas" Masumoto began in 2002 when his series of monthly "letters" began appearing in the *Fresno Bee*. I was a staff artist at the time and was asked to create a distinctive illustrative approach that would complement Mas' writing. After four years I still relish the ongoing opportunity to create watercolor paintings for each new essay. For that opportunity I thank publisher Ray Steele, former executive editor Charlie Waters, and editorial page editor Jim Boren.

Each month I look forward to my visit to the newsroom to deliver my artwork. I have great respect for all the journalists at the *Fresno Bee*. I'd particularly like to mention the individuals I work most closely with: associate editor Gail Marshall, art director Andrea Cooper, and editorial staff artists S. W. Parra and Yen Vang. It's an honor to be welcomed by this community of professionals.

My life continues to be enriched by my professional and personal relationship with Mas. I admire the breadth of his interests and his inclusive vision of life in the "other California." It feels like a little holiday to me every time I drive the twenty or so miles to the Masumoto farm; the experience invigorates me as well as my work. He and his family are generous and welcoming. The pictures I've made of his home have come to feel like pictures of my home too.

I am gratified that Heyday Books publisher Malcolm Margolin recognizes and nurtures the author and artist's creative synthesis of words and pictures. It pleases me that a wider audience is discovering our vision of the San Joaquin Valley. I thank designer Lorraine Rath and everyone else at Heyday for this gem of a book.

Finally, I express my gratitude to all the readers who have made *Heirlooms* and its companion, *Letters to the Valley*, a part of their world.

—Doug Hansen

Great Valley Books

Great Valley Books is a program of Heyday Institute, Berkeley. Books in the Great Valley series strive to publish, promote, and develop a deep appreciation of various aspects of the region's unique history and culture. Created in 2002 with a grant from The James Irvine Foundation, it strives to promote the rich literary, artistic, and cultural resources of California's Central Valley by publishing books of the highest merit and broadest interest.

A few of our Great Valley Books and other Central Valley titles include:

Blithe Tomato, by Mike Madison; *Haslam's Valley*, by Gerald Haslam; *Highway 99: A Literary Journey through California's Great Central Valley*, edited by Stan Yogi; *Skin Tax*, by Tim Hernandez; and *Letters to the Valley: A Harvest of Memories*, by David Mas Masumoto.

For more a complete list of Great Valley Books titles and information, please visit our website at www.heydaybooks.com/public/greatvalley.html.

GREAT
VALLEY